Abolish the Family

Abolish the Family

A Manifesto for Care and Liberation

Sophie Lewis

VERSO

London • New York

I, the broom, dedicate this book to
the West Philadelphia cemetery commune.

First published by Verso 2022
© Sophie Lewis 2022

1 3 5 7 9 10 8 6 4 2

Verso
UK: 6 Meard Street, London W1F 0EG
US: 388 Atlantic Avenue, Brooklyn, NY 11217
versobooks.com

Verso is the imprint of New Left Books

ISBN-13: 978-1-83976-719-7
ISBN-13: 978-1-83976-721-0 (US EBK)
ISBN-13: 978-1-83976-720-3 (UK EBK)

British Library Cataloguing in Publication Data
A catalogue record for this book is available from the British Library

Library of Congress Cataloging-in-Publication Data
A catalog record for this book is available from the Library of Congress

Typeset in Sabon by Hewer Text UK Ltd, Edinburgh
Printed and bound by CPI Group (UK) Ltd, Croydon, CR0 4YY

Contents

But I Love My Family!

"There are other ways of naming each other as relations."
—Tiffany Lethabo King[1]

Abolish the family? You might as well abolish gravity or abolish god. So! The left is trying to take grandma away, now, and confiscate kids, and this is supposed to be progressive? What the fuck!?

Many people experience a reaction something like this, upon first encountering the phrase "abolish the family." And that's okay. I will neither deny nor shy away from the slogan's explosive emotional freight. My purpose in it is partly, to be sure, to clarify and correct the many possible *aghast* misapprehensions one can easily form about family abolition; for example, that it means forcibly separating people. But ultimately, I don't want to deny that there is something "scary" (psychologically challenging) about this politics. This same scariness is present in all real revolutionary politics, in my view. Our trepidation is our reflexive response to the premonition of an abolition of the *self*.[2] All of us—even those of us who own no property, who receive no guaranteed care, and who subsist at the blunt end of empire, whiteness, cis-hetero-patriarchy, and class—will have to let go of *something* as the process of our collective liberation unfolds. If the world is to be remade utterly, then a person must be willing to be remade also. We sense this. And it is difficult, perhaps impossible, right now, to imagine *not* being manufactured through the private nuclear household and the oedipal kinship story (mother figure, father figure, child). Yet personhood was not always created this way, which means we could, if we wanted to, create it *otherwise*. In the meantime, if your kneejerk reaction to the words "abolish the family" is "but I love my family," you ought to know that you are one of the lucky ones. And I am happy for you. But everyone should be so lucky, don't you think?

Loving the people in your family, mind you, is not at odds with a commitment to family abolition. Quite the reverse. I will hazard a definition of love: to love a person is to struggle for their autonomy as well as for their immersion in care, insofar such abundance is possible in a world choked by capital. If this is true, then restricting the number of mothers (of whatever gender) to whom a child has access, on the basis that I am the "real" mother, is not necessarily a form of love worthy of the name. Perchance, when you were very young (assuming you grew up in a nuclear household), you quietly noticed the oppressiveness of the function assigned to whoever was the mother in your home. You sensed her loneliness. You felt a twinge of solidarity. In my experience, children often "get" this better than most: when you love someone, it simply makes no sense to endorse a social technology that isolates them, privatizes their lifeworld, arbitrarily assigns their dwelling-place, class, and very identity in law, and drastically circumscribes their sphere of intimate, interdependent ties. But I am getting ahead of myself.

Most family abolitionists love their families. It is true of course that it is usually the people who have had bad experiences within a social system, and who feel things *besides* love for that system, who initiate movements to overthrow it. But loving one's family in spite of a "hard childhood" is pretty typical of the would-be family abolitionist. She may, for instance, sense in her gut that she and the members of her family simply aren't *good* for each other, while also loving them, wishing them joy, and knowing full well that there are *few or no* available alternatives in this world when it comes to providing much-needed care for everybody in question. Frankly, loving one's family can be a problem *for anyone*. It might put extra weights around the ankles of a domestic battery survivor seeking to escape (especially given the economic punishments imposed by capitalism on those who flee commodified housing). It might hinder a trans or disabled child from claiming medical care. It might dissuade someone from getting an abortion. Right now, few would deny that reproductive *rights*—let alone justice—are everywhere systematically denied to populations. Austerity policies purposively render proletarian baby-making crushingly unaffordable, even for two or three or four adults working together, let alone one. Housework is sexed, racialized, and (except in the houses of the rich) unwaged. It is unsurprising, in these global conditions, that large numbers of humans do not or *cannot* love their families. Reasons range from simple incompatibility to various phobias, ableism, sexual violence, and neglect.

Let me tell you a secret: people get really angry when you suggest to them that they deserved better than what they got growing up. And I've noticed that a lot of people have the "*but I love my family*" reaction with the most startling vehemence immediately after they've spent a long time talking freely to me about the strain, tragedy, blackmail, and care-starved frustration that characterized their "biological" upbringing. Angry opposition to the idea that *things could be different* comes, I've found, right after we have voiced the wish that relatives of ours could have been less alone, less burdened by caring responsibilities, less trapped. Those people are quite another matter, this defensive spasm seems to say: I, myself, don't need any family abolition, thank you very much. Sure, it may be a disciplinary, scarcity-based trauma-machine: but it's MY disciplinary, scarcity-based trauma-machine.

Listen. I get it. It's not just that you're worried about your dad getting all upset if he sees you with this book. It's that it's existentially petrifying to imagine relinquishing the organized poverty we have in favor of an abundance we have never known and have yet to organize.

What is the family? So deep runs the idea that the family is the exclusive place where people are safe, where people come from, where people are made, and where people belong, it doesn't even feel like an idea anymore. Let us unpick it, then.

The family is the reason we are supposed to want to go to work, the reason we have to go to work, and the reason we *can* go to work. It is, at root, the name we use for the fact that care is privatized in our society. And because it feels synonymous with care, "family" is every civic-minded individual's raison d'être par excellence: an ostensibly non-individualist creed and unselfish principle to which one voluntarily signs up without thinking about it. What alternative could there be? The economic assumption that behind every "breadwinner" there is a private someone (or someones) worth being exploited for, notably some kind of wife—that is, a person who is likely a breadwinner too—"freely" making sandwiches with the hard-won bread, or hiring someone else to do so, vacuuming up the crumbs, and refrigerating leftovers, such that more bread can be won tomorrow: this feels to many of us like a description of "human nature."

Without the family, who or what would take responsibility for the lives of non-workers, including the ill, the young, and the elderly? This question is a bad one. We don't hesitate to say that nonhuman animals are better off outside of zoos, even if alternative habitats for them are growing scarcer and scarcer and, moreover, they have become used to the abusive care of zoos. Similarly: transition out of the family will be tricky, yes, but the family is doing a bad job at care, and we all deserve better. The family is getting in the way of alternatives.

In part, the vertiginous question "what's the alternative?" arises because it is not just the *worker* (and her work) that the family gives birth to every day, in theory. The family is also the legal assertion that a baby, a neonatal human, is the creation of the familial romantic dyad; and that this act of authorship in turn generates, for the authors, property rights in "their" progeny—*parenthood*—but also quasi-exclusive accountability for the child's life. The near-total dependence of the young person on these guardians is portrayed not as the harsh lottery that it patently is, but rather as "natural," not in need of social mitigation, and, furthermore, *beautiful* for all concerned. Children, it is proposed, benefit from having only one or two parents and, at best, a few other "second-ary" caregivers. Parents, it is supposed, derive nothing so much as joy from the romance of this isolated intensity. Constant allusions to the hellworld of sheer exhaustion parents inhabit notwithstanding, their condition is senti-mentalized to the nth degree: it is downright taboo to regret parenthood. All too seldom is parenthood identified as an absurdly unfair distribution of labor, and a despotic distribution of responsibility for and power over younger people. A distribution that could be changed.

Like a microcosm of the nation-state, the family incu-bates chauvinism and competition. Like a factory with a billion branches, it manufactures "individuals" with a cultural, ethnic, and binary gender identity; a class; and a racial consciousness. Like an infinitely renewable energy source, it performs free labor for the market. Like an "organic element of historical progress," writes Anne McClintock in *Imperial Leather*, it worked for imperial-ism as an image of *hierarchy-within-unity* that grew "indispensable for legitimating exclusion and hierarchy" in general.[3] For all these reasons, the family functions as capitalism's base unit—in Mario Mieli's phrase, "the cell of the social tissue."[4] It may be easier to imagine the end of capitalism, as I've riffed elsewhere, than the end of the family. But everyday utopian experiments *do* generate strands of an altogether different social tissue: micro-cultures which could be scaled up if the movement for a classless society took seriously the premise that house-holds can be formed freely and run democratically; the principle that no one shall be deprived of food, shelter, or care because they don't work.

Family values are bourgeois economics writ small. As Melinda Cooper demonstrates, under the sign of the family, starting in the late seventies, neoliberals and neoconservatives both essentially reinvented welfare along Elizabethan "poor law" principles: rendering kin, instead of society, responsible for the poor. Even in the original legislation four hundred years ago, concepts like "market freedom," "the liberal individual," and debt were slowly erected on the plinths of kinship obligations and family bonds. Without family, in short, no bourgeois state. The family's function is to replace welfare and to guarantee debtors. Masquerading as the choice, creation, and desire of individuals, the family is a method for cheaply arranging the reproduction of the nation's labor-power and securing debt repayments.

But wait, the family is in danger!—or so legend has it. *Kids these days, they won't procreate, they don't look after their folks, they live at home, they don't call home, they don't aspire to homeownership, they won't marry, they don't put family first, and they aren't founding families.* Guess what? The family has never not been critically at risk. As Cooper puts it in the opening sentence of *Family Values: Between Neoliberalism and the New Social Conservatism*, "The history of the family is one of perpetual crisis."[5] Imminent collapse is an integral part of the deal, although look around, and you'll quickly notice, reports of the death of the family have been greatly exaggerated. To attack the family is as unthinkable in liberal-democratic politics as it has ever been. Nowhere on the party-political spectrum can one find proposals to dethrone the family, hasten its demise, or even decenter it in policy.

"Family values" and Politics—with a capital "P"—have long been synonyms. When Margaret Thatcher, the "milk snatcher" of the eighties, said "*There is no such thing as society, there are individual men and women and there are families*," she wasn't so much (alas) winning an argument against anti-family foes as triumphally making a capitalist reality explicit. That which is "social" is not simply anti-profitability but anti-family, she implies. The family—that is, the family *shop* or *seed fund*—is the great anti-social institution. And indeed, in a landscape laid to waste by Thatcherite anti-solidarity policies, it really can feel as though there are *only families*, or races (macro-families), at war with one another or, at best, in competition.[6] Taxes, benefits, wills, deeds, curricula, courts, and pensions are everywhere at work, functioning as technologies of the family. Even at the architectural level, a visiting stranger in such a land faces an endless sea of front doors—each neatly attached to a mortgage and a (real or implied) "Private" sign, each harboring its micro-collection of individual self-managing consumer-entrepreneurs. Meanwhile, most public or common spaces are not only dedicated to commercial leisure, but designed to cater pointedly to the couple-form or the nuclear brood.

And yet, even as the family, as a mode of governance, is a brutal economic fact, the family *as a lived experience* remains a bit of a fiction. Not very many human beings actually live in one—and/but this doesn't matter. Millions of us cohabit in ad-hoc, odd, creative, warehoused, forced or partially communalized ways; further millions upon millions live entirely alone. It doesn't make a difference, though, because, at the same time as seeming chosen and optional, the family consigns those outside its frame to social illegibility. All of us are seduced, or at least disciplined. We can't escape it, even when we individually reject it. And even when we reject it, we worry that its much-vaunted disintegration presages something worse.

Everybody loses. For all purposes except capital accumulation, the promise of family falls abjectly short of itself. Often, this is nobody's "fault" per se: simply, too much is being asked of too few. On the other hand, the family is where most of the rape happens on this earth, and most of the murder. No one is likelier to rob, bully, blackmail, manipulate, or hit you, or inflict unwanted touch, than family. Logically, announcing an intention to "treat you like family" (as so many airlines, restaurants, banks, retailers, and workplaces do) ought to register as a horrible threat. Instead, to be metaphorically "family" in someone's eyes makes-believe that one has something quite ... *unfamilial*. Namely: acceptance, solidarity, an open promise of help, welcome, and care.

Of course, the administrative grid of the family does organize where certain forms of help (are legally obligated to) come from. But this has nothing to do with solidarity. The family—predicated on the privatization of that which should be common, and on proprietary concepts of couple, blood, gene, and seed—is a state institution, not a popular organism. It's at once a normative aspiration and a last resort: a blackmail passing itself off as fate; a shitty contract pretending to be biological necessity. Think about how (on TV, or in your own life) a *reminder* of family ties and obligations is often a cruelly repressive move. Think about how, in mafia movies, loyalty to and love for "the family" is enforced among members via penalties worse than death—and this only feels like a mobster exaggeration of the general, civilian logic of the family. Think about the British royal family and the deadly logics of eugenicism, lovelessness, and property-worship that govern its internal affairs, even as it is held up as a prototype for the family around the world and exoticized (albeit criticized) for an international audience on the ongoing 2016 Netflix series *The Crown*. Think about honor killings, femicides, and the deaths of children like English six-year-old Arthur Labinjo-Hughes, whose murderers, in the words of Richard Seymour, "thought they were his victims."[7]

How, given all this, does the family still serve as the standard for all other relational possibilities? I don't know: perhaps because, to quote Seymour again, the family "can be, though it isn't necessarily, the heart of a heartless world."[8] I suspect the religion of family revolves around this glowing hope that it *will* be. We are grasping at a chance of guaranteed belonging, trust, recognition, and fulfillment. The family dream is our dream of a haven—the very opposite of hunger or straitjackets. Idiomatically, to say that someone is "like family" is meant to convey in the strongest possible terms: "I claim you, I love you. I consider our fates bound up together." We have no stronger metaphor! But why use *this* metaphor?

Tolstoy famously opened his magnum opus with the truthy formula "All happy families are alike; unhappy families are each unhappy in their own way." It sounds good, concedes Ursula K. Le Guin: "It's a great first sentence."[9] So many families are extremely unhappy! And this extreme unhappiness feels unique, because its structural character—like the structure of capitalism—is cunningly obscured from view.

In fact, Le Guin suggests, the reverse of Tolstoy's apothegm is ultimately closer to the truth. She knows of what she speaks, having herself grown up "in a family

that on the whole seems to have been happier than most."
She finds it "false—an intolerable cheapening of reality—
simply to describe it as happy." To her, the very phrase
"happy families" bespeaks a fundamental incuriosity
about the nature of happiness, which—under capitalism
especially—comes with enormous costs. Those who
breezily deploy it forget that there is a "whole substruc-
ture of sacrifices, repressions, suppressions, choices made
or forgone, chances taken or lost, balancings of greater
and lesser evils," at the foundation of familial happiness.
They ignore "the tears, the fears, the migraines, the injus-
tices, the censorships, the quarrels, the lies, the angers,
the cruelties." Yes, families can be happy, Le Guin main-
tains, poker-faced and only possibly joking, "for quite a
long time—a week, a month, even longer." The happy
families Tolstoy "speaks of so confidently in order to
dismiss them as all alike," though?—"where are they?"
What if *unhappy* families are all alike, in a structural
sense, because *the* family is a miserable way to organize
care—whereas happy ones are miraculous anomalies?

As a child, I used to play a card game called "Happy
Families" with the other members of my far-from-happy
nuclear family. The deck was illustrated in 1851. Each set
bears a name like Pots, Bun, Dose, and Tape, and has four
components: a male head of the household (who plies his
trade: painting, baking, doctoring, tailoring), one wife
(who helps him), and two children, representing both
binary gender options—boy and girl. *Dad: may I have
Master Bung, the Brewer's Son?* I'd ask, guessing a card I
wanted, hidden in my target opponent's hand. If I had
guessed correctly, I claimed the card, with the Bung Boy's
grotesque portrait on it, and then asked for another, and
another: *Thank you! Now, Mum, may I have Mrs. Grits,*

the Grocer's Wife? Much obliged. Now, Mum again: may I have Miss Dip, the Dyer's Daughter? It was great fun; devilish. I recall the gleeful vindictiveness of the game, above all (or alternatively: droll, powerless dismay). Until one makes an error and cedes control, one is on a roll, imperiously stripping the cards from everyone's hands in a triumphal progress of family-reunification. *Boom, that's the Boneses complete.* It's their togetherness, I suppose, that makes the happiness. Could it work for us? We, the players, were generationally and gender-apportioned in the same quartet—Dad, Mum, Ben, and me.

The sensibility in "Happy Families" is refreshingly mocking (the individuals depicted are all daft, nasty, pathetic, ridiculous, vain-looking characters). At the same time, the game evokes a powerful fantasy: every human being is in her cosmically pre-destined place in a perfectly symmetrical genealogical grid. Barbers beget little barbers, who grow up to marry, what else, barbers' wives, and so they beget more barbers in turn. Each person inherits an economic vocation—the family's natural business—that presumably harmonizes perfectly with the wider Happy Society's ecology of useful trades. All the Dips have dye on their happy hands, not just Mr. Dip. All four of the Soots are sooty. And clearly Miss Soot, with her duster, has no thought in her head of ever being something other than the Daughter of the Sweep (except, one day, no doubt, a different dustman's wife). The conflation of the individual and the family is absolute, as is the conflation of the family and the family *business*. Members of society who do not *work* are unthinkable within the famous card-deck's schema. "This is a fantasy of an economy," to quote what Michèle Barrett and Mary McIntosh had to say about family ideology in the eighties, "in which the actions of self-seeking 'economic men' add up, through the 'unseen hand' of the market mechanism, to an optimal pattern of production and consumption."[10]

Lo and behold, decades later, in 2021, the best-selling author and economist Emily Oster published *The Family Firm*, a "data-driven" handbook for "running your family like a business." Oster's book unironically assesses the "human resources" dynamics of the private bourgeois home vis-à-vis the wider economy, all the while providing a handy "management" toolkit for the would-be competitive player in today's fast-paced parenting decisionscape. "How much extra happiness will more money buy you?" Oster proposes asking yourself during a budget meeting. "It's worth considering not just the *number* of dollars but the *marginal utility* of those dollars."[11] You may, as a parent, decide that happiness lies in working less and spending more time with the kids, but the rationale for this, in Oster's matrix, still makes its way inexorably back to productivity: "I value that time," she vouchsafes, "in part to get to hang out with them and, honestly, in part because I do not think anyone else is tough enough on supervising violin practice."

The family is an ideology of work. In the early twenty-first century, as Oster shamelessly details, its credo has become the optimization (via violin-playing and other forms of so-called human capital investment) of a population of high-earning, flexible entrepreneurs. Previously, as we saw, the workers crafted by the family were imagined more along the lines of the trades-guild avatars depicted on the "Happy Families" playing-cards: Mr. Chip or Mr. Bung (a petty bourgeois earner) and his hardworking but unwaged wife and children. Indeed, ever since the European labor movement *won* the male-breadwinner household for itself in the 1890s, socialists have cleaved to the romantic idea of the working-class "provider" whose dependent nest-mates (grandpa, grandma, woman, brats, unwed sister-in-law) are all happily identified with what he does by way of work.[12] Today, Mr. Waitress, in contrast, will probably re-train at least twice—becoming Mr. Tech Support, Mr. Nurse, Mr. Uber Eats, and so on, sometimes all at the same time. In the so-called advanced or overdeveloped economies which academics like to call "feminized" (on account of the higher proportion of female workers employed, but also the traditional "gender"—service, hospitality, support, computing, affect—of the key profit sectors) almost everyone has to try to be a "male breadwinner." From this precarious vantagepoint, there is something attractive, pseudo-utopian even, about the fictive Miss Soot's perfect absence of anxiety about who she is. To be a "working family," an artisanal team ordained by the cosmos itself, is a deeply seductive idea; an evocation of security, of harmony, and "right reproduction." No wonder consumers, voters and pundits love the notion of a "family business," a "mom 'n' pop shop," despite clear evidence that workers' wages, benefits and working conditions are worse, not better, within such establishments.

Emily Oster might be an exception to this claim, but it seems to me that capitalist societies, once they'd invented family values (that is, *work* values), on the whole failed to advance them with a consistently straight face. Everybody knows that not everybody (to put it mildly) experiences the family as a blissful state; that not everybody (to put it mildly) loves their work. Some of us have always known. To be sure, humorless, straightforward, quasi-fascist paeans to the heteronormative hearth and the aspirational industriousness it breeds exist in great numbers, from sentimental Victorian fiction to patriotic Hollywood thrillers and, increasingly, Christian-nationalist policy platforms. But an overwhelming amount of equally mainstream art and literature is also about family ideology's "discontents." Anti-family politics isn't unthinkable, in other words—it's everywhere! Art and writing about family life is usually at the very least satirical, and often downright dark. Think of *King Lear, Tristram Shandy, Jane Eyre, Middlemarch, Madame Bovary, Beloved, Twin Peaks, The Sopranos, Game of Thrones, Breaking Bad, The Simpsons*, or Alison Bechdel's *Fun Home*, to name only the first (forgive me) "household names" that come to my mind. Realist and gothic traditions alike view family as a field of howling boredom, aching lack, unhealed trauma, unspeakable secrets, buried hurts, wronged ghosts, "knives out," torture attics, and peeling wallpaper. Yet in "cli fi" and related representations of national emergencies and the apocalypse, authors insist on family as the core relationship we will *need* to rely on, when all else is stripped away.[13]

It bears spelling out that satire does not by itself unsettle power, and probably sometimes offers the consolations of "relatability" *instead of* inciting audiences to mount a less-tolerant response to what they see. Yet the fact that culture routinely questions the morality of work—and shines a light on the nihilism of the precept "family first"—*matters*. It matters that admitting how disappointing family life is—how irksome, unjust, and exhausting at best, and crushingly traumatic at worst—represents one of the dominant established tones of the classical novel, family cartoon, drama, sitcom, and memoir. Sure enough, familiality and coupledom are sometimes satirized so subtly one can barely tell. Such moves are in themselves canonical: the happily-ever-after "script" subjected to heart-felt critiques by the characters in a novel or mini-series, only to then unfold anyway (to the characters' delighted surprise and bemused embarrassment!) for a plot resolution of maybe-this-time-it'll-be-different quiescence. "Down with love" is never the conclusion of a narrative: it is, however, sometimes the view espoused by our heroes at the beginning. The literarily self-aware characters in a Sally Rooney novel know all of this. When one semi-serious answer to the question *Beautiful World, Where Are You* turns out to be: *in the bosom of the conventional family you have decided to form with your childhood sweetheart*, there is no doubt: the novel is trolling us![14] Yet readers still consume the experience of political and existential anguish melting away as Alice and Felix and Eileen and Simon stop worrying about capitalism and embrace their desire to marry.

Genres of family critique other than the bourgeois novel do exist, but they aren't necessarily pretty. I'm thinking of the medium crawling with moms turned murderers, blood-spattered dining-rooms, incest revenges, and homes set ablaze: *Hereditary, The Shining, Society, Goodnight Mommy, Psycho, The Stepfather, Us*. Critical cinema scholars have long identified a latently insurrectionary desire at play in horror movies, especially those that depict attacks (often from within) on the propertied white family, the patriarchal regime of housework, or the colonial homestead.[15] Books like *Hearths of Darkness: The Family in the American Horror Film* argue that violent and scary movie-making is, more often than not, a popular vehicle for mass anti-family desire.[16] Think of the menacing domestic interiors, hostile kitchen appliances, creepy children, murderous kin, and claustrophobic hellscapes of your favorite horror flick. In slasher, home-invasion, and feminist horror canons, the narrative pretends to worry nationalistically about external threats to the family while, in fact, indulging every conceivable fantasy of dismembering and setting fire to it from within. From gore to so-called "psychological" horror, diverse genres openly implicate the family-form in the tortures it is enduring. In these movies, the suppressed, disavowed violence of the home is returning home. The monster is coming from inside the house.

Wow, who am I calling *monsters*—dads and moms and great-aunt Trish? No: family abolition is not "puerile" politics (albeit children must be on the front lines of imagining it). Family abolition does not expect a state of perfect, uninterrupted, universal happiness. Rather, I would ask you to flip the script and consider that it is *the family* that is unrealistic and utopian. The family, right now, is supposed to make everybody happy. We are all supposed to be avatars of our little biological team of competitive social reproduction. When we are delinquent, we are a burden on the family: an experience which, ideally, reforms us by making us remember (like it's a good thing) that family is all we've got. Even when we are exceptional, we are, in a sense, chips off our biogenetic clan's block; something for blood relations to be proud of.

Modern familialism is not so far off from the psychology of Miss Soot as we might like to think. It's as though we've forgotten that her happiness, like *her very name*, is a self-conscious fiction. To make the flesh-and-blood Misses Soot of this world happy—*truly* happy—we have to accept that human beings are actualized neither in work nor in reproduction. We have to find out one another's real names and struggle together against the system that makes arbitrary data on birth certificates shape people's fates. It should be elementary socialism, not some fringe eccentricity of queer ultra-leftists, to be striving toward a regime of cohabitation, collective eating, leisure, eldercare, and childrearing in which no one, to quote M. E. O'Brien, "is bound together violently any longer,"[17] like sets in a ghoulish deck of playing-cards.

I'd wager that you, too, can imagine something better than the lottery that drops a neonate arbitrarily among one or two or three or four individuals (of a particular class) and keeps her there for the best part of two decades without her consent, making her wholly beholden to them for her physical survival, legal existence, and economic identity, and forcing her to be the reason they give away their lives in work. I'd wager that you, too, can imagine something better than the norm that makes a prison for adults—especially women—out of their own commitment to children they love. Together, we can invent accounts of human "nature," and ways of organizing social reproduction, that are not just economic contracts with the state, or worker training programs in disguise. Together, we can establish consensus-based modes of transgenerational cohabitation, and large-scale methods for distributing and minimizing the burdens of life's work.

Even then, I seriously doubt we will have found the *blueprints for happiness*. Ursula K. Le Guin's question still gives me tingles, though: those happy families Tolstoy was so uninterested in, *where are they*? Contrary to the trendy cynicism and faux-radical realism of the canonical litterateurs who considered misery to be somehow *truer* than happiness, Le Guin treats happiness as the rarer, more interesting, more pressing, challenging collective artform. Family abolition, she might agree with me, is an important vehicle for such curiosity about—and desire for—happiness.

Those of us assigned to so-called reproductive labors on this earth know especially well that happiness is a clumsy art, a Sisyphean effort, a messy choreography that, by definition, cannot leave anybody out. No doubt, a world in which most members of most households are deeply and truly happy most of the time lies mostly in the future, part of a yet-to-be-written history. It feels like the horizon toward which speculative fictions like Le Guin's are reaching. But like all utopias, too, that world already nestles latently in the present. It has its wispy sprouts in nooks and crannies wherever people, against all odds, are seeking to devise liberatory and queer—which is to say, anti-property—modes of care. (The word "queer" has widely been emptied of its communist meanings, yet here and there, and certainly in this writer's heart, it still carries some abolitionist freight, signifying resistance to capitalism's reproductive institutions: marriage, private property, patriarchy, the police, school.) Queerly, then, the best care-givers already seek to unmake the kind of *possessive love* Alexandra Kollontai called "property love" in their relations with children, older relatives, and partners. The comradeliest mother-ers already seek to deprivatize care. So, in a strict sense it may be true, as Michael Hardt asserts, that the production of real happiness is doomed under current conditions: "only once property love is abolished can we begin to invent a new love, a revolutionary love, a red love."[18] But it also seems indisputable that many of us are getting on with the abolishing.

As we'll shortly see, the idea of abolishing the family is very old (Plato wrote *The Republic* around 375 BC; and Charles Fourier first imagined "feminism" and the "phalanstery" two hundred years ago). There have been certain periods, including the sixties and seventies, when relatively many people were familiar with it. In a minute, in chapter 3, we'll dig into the history of family abolitionism, which includes nineteenth-century French utopians, Marx and Engels's "infamous proposal," thwarted Bolshevik commissars like Kollontai, revolutionary feminists like Shulamith Firestone, mid-century Gay Power activists and children's liberationists, rowdy welfare recipients, queer Indigenous and Black militants, and twenty-first century trans Marxists. But before this potted history, our attention will turn—in chapter 2—to the pros and cons of opting for the (unnecessarily inflammatory, some say) terminology of "abolition" as opposed to the available alternatives: "reform," "expand," and so on. What does abolition even mean, in this context? Should family abolitionists take pains to specify that they mean the "white" or "bourgeois" or "nuclear" family— not, perish the thought, *your* complex, financially struggling, queer and/or racially marginalized kinship network? Or should we insist that there is no family other than the white, nuclear, bourgeois family, in a structural sense? To answer this, we dig into the differences between white ruling-class and, on the other hand, Black proletarian (or colonized) people's relationships to the family. Why might it make sense to describe "the Black family" as an oxymoron? Why do some people reject the idea that "abolishing the family" is desirable for nonwhite groups and oppressed classes? Is calling for family abolition compatible with treasuring techniques and traditions of mutual survival developed by colonized, or formerly enslaved, people? Finally, in chapter 4, I consider what a movement of *real families against the family* might look like, and then make an argument for going beyond that metaphor: letting go of kinship altogether and pushing forward the relations we might call comradeship, or kith, or words that have not been invented yet.

2

Abolish Which Family?

"Although our families may have taken a somewhat different form from that of whites, the socialization that was necessary to maintain the state was carried out."

—"The Black Woman as a Woman,"
Kay Lindsey, 1970

At this juncture, perhaps you are thinking, okay, this is all very well, but the term "abolish" seems provocative and toxic in this context, not to mention needlessly misleading in 2022. Come on, we don't want to do with families what we want to do with prisons, do we? Certainly not Black and brown and Indigenous and/or queer working-class families! Isn't family abolition (especially without the "white family" or "bourgeois" qualifier), when we really get down to it, a fantastical indulgence for relatively affluent white socialists or queer settlers or at least atheist feminists at the imperial core? Otherwise, how could one possibly talk about "abolishing the family" in, say, a Palestinian organizing context, in which the indigenous family is always already pre-abolished by the genocidal occupying power? How can one say "abolish the family" to the detainees in refugee camps, separated purposively from their kinfolk, fleeing El Salvador, Guatemala, Sudan, Colombia, Syria, Yemen, Afghanistan? In what sense would one expect LGBT people to sign up to an agenda that sounds like a demand to forgo access to the same hospital kin-visitation rights and procreative technologies straight people have? Perhaps it would be better to call for an *expanded* family, or a *reformed* version of the family, rather than an abolished one. It makes no sense to run the risk of appearing to compare the downsides of colonized people's kinship practices with ... the carceral state. Surely it is reckless to seek to defend a politics that might be construed as saying that families—the *very thing* that often works tirelessly to protect Black, migrant, and Indigenous youth from violence, hiding them from cops and freeing them from jails, and so on—are equivalent somehow to their enemies: cops, courts, and jails.

As you can see, I'm semi-fluent—almost impassioned—when it comes to reeling out points against becoming a partisan of "family abolition." They are compelling, these counterarguments, even to me. Since publishing *Full Surrogacy Now*, they have given me pause and stretched my thinking, spawning too many discussions to count. Even now, I am almost persuaded that saying "abolish the family" is too risky, too unstrategic, utopian in the wrong sense of the word. I am *almost* persuaded, but not quite: which is why, in this chapter, I will do my best to mount a case for a critically utopianist position, assembling arguments from Hortense Spillers, Tiffany Lethabo King, Jennifer Nash, Hazel Carby, Paul Gilroy, Kathi Weeks, Kay Lindsey, Lola Olufemi, and Annie Olaloku-Teriba. As all these teachers of mine know, there have been noxious white versions of family abolitionism in the past. And there remain bad white versions of soi-disant "family abolition" discourse now. (Some such came out of the woodwork under the lockdowns of the COVID-19 era, as it happens. On social media, I observed, a small number of privileged women and young queers briefly appropriated this radical terminology to rail against physical distancing and shelter-in-place directives, resenting being deprived of the domestic help and of queer sexual freedom, respectively. From what I saw, the blips in question were rightly teased, chided, and refuted.)

For well over a century, as we will see in the next chapter, socialists, feminists, and revolutionaries in the United States have argued over the best orientation to take toward forms of family that aren't (or at least don't seem to be) bourgeois or white. The fight hit the mainstream when, in 1965, the US secretary of labor officially diagnosed the (female-led) "Negro family" as "a tangle of pathology," galvanizing an entire critical tradition back into action. In the thirties, Black socialist sociologists like E. Franklin Frazier had set out to discover—and appropriate for the purposes of a politics of Black respectability—a true pastoral Black family within the archive of slavery. Naturally, the violently anti-Black Moynihan report revived this tradition. This time around, though, a skeptical left-feminist counter-tradition emerged, too, which peaked with philosopher Hortense Spillers's epochal account of the production of Black un-motherhood in ante-bellum America, "Mama's Baby, Papa's Maybe." Unimpressed with the reconciliatory misogyny embedded in pro-Black protestations (like Frazier's) that enslaved people had always aspired to the patriarchal family as best they could—with the implication that, hence, their descendants can and will uphold it—Spillers wanted to take the violently produced "kinlessness" of Black people seriously enough to necessitate the crafting of a whole new kin-equivalent way of relating.

She writes: "Whether or not we decide that the support systems that African-Americans derived under conditions of captivity should be called 'family,' or something else, strikes me as supremely impertinent." The point, for Spillers, is that "African peoples in the historic Diaspora had nothing to prove," given that it is "stunningly evident" that they were capable of modes of care "at least as complex as those of the 'nuclear family' in the West." Rather than orienting toward the "family" as a measuring-stick (or aspiration), Spillers focuses on the fact that Black women in the wake of slavery stand "*out* of the traditional symbolics of female gender," and what this means for political struggle—namely: "it is our task to make a place for this different social subject." A place, in other words, that one might call a family, or not. So, whereas Frazier's "good revisionist history" (as Spillers acidly calls it) of "The Negro Family" is ironically quite close to Moynihan's—both agree that a "matriarchate" is something obscene—Spillers discards both options, proposing that the existing "grammar" of American life is unfit for purpose, especially for Black women: "We are less interested in joining the ranks of gendered femaleness than gaining the *insurgent* ground as female social subject."[1]

Spillers's text can be read as family-abolitionist, and Tiffany Lethabo King does read it that way in a 2018 essay, to great effect.[2] But apart from "Mama's Baby, Papa's Maybe," King notes, Black scholarly and feminist/womanist responses to the Moynihan report rarely go this far; "rarely [do they] interrogate the viability of the notion of the family itself." Rather, arguments are typically made for "expanded," "extended," "non-sanguinal," "queer," and "intergenerational" alternatives. The problem, for King, with these "modifications and revisions to the family" is that they "still retain attachments to the liberal humanistic concept of the filial,"[3] meaning that they refer back to the human "subject" of liberalism who has *not* been ungendered via slavery, and so don't quite break free of the definition of kinship (*kinship-as-property-relation*) that Spillers, in the eighties, exposed as elemental to white American culture (its racial/gender *grammar*).

The rubric of Black motherhood, for those of us who would defend it against the necropolitical forces that crush and denigrate it, inspires celebratory, even ecstatic queer-utopian theorization. As a result, it has to be said, we don't always leave ourselves much room to challenge possible patriarchal and proprietary violences *by* mothers (of any gender) within Black families, or room to note the violence that the celebratory model potentially does to those mothers themselves. The 2016 anthology *Revolutionary Mothering* co-edited by Gumbs, Martens and Williams—which seeks to queer the expanded-Black-kinship field associated with Carol Stack's touchstone ethnography, *All Our Kin* (1974)[4]—oscillates between revaluing devalued motherhoods in a language of queer euphoria, and flirting with the idea that, while mother*ing* is revolutionary, mother*hood* is part of what has to go. Rereading the anthology recently with Tiffany Lethabo King's perspective in mind, I reflected on how tenaciously the family, as a naturalized form of human organization, persists in the shadow—*as* the shadow—of its beautiful alternates. I feel deep appreciation for *Revolutionary Mothering*, which has changed my life and, in their own words, the lives of several of my students. Lately I've been wondering, though, if we can go further.

So, it seems, has the theorist of sexuality Jennifer Nash, who recently applied her critical powers to the subject of Black motherhood specifically, including in an essay reviewing *Revolutionary Mothering*. "As a black feminist scholar," Nash confesses carefully, "I remain both seduced by and skeptical of the representation of black motherhood as radical and revolutionary, as spiritual and transformative."[5] Contemporary visionaries like Alexis Pauline Gumbs are building the knowledge that "Black mothering is queer"[6] on strong foundations laid by that earlier giant of queer studies Cathy Cohen (who proposed to combat the defanging of queerness by tethering it to "Punks, Bulldaggers and Welfare Queens"). But even when welfare austerity and prisons are centered in the analytic frame—as mentioned—I don't know if the discourses we tend to assemble under the headers "queer," "Black," and "reproductive justice" help us to name oppressive structures that queer Black mothering milieus themselves, or queer Black mothers themselves, might be upholding.

Revolutionaries must welcome and enable potential challenges *from within*—challenges from children, for example, who may have their own ideas about how to be in relation, or from women who do not feel that their mothering (or refusal of mothering) has yet reached the level of revolutionary. We must hear the grown women, non-binary people, and men who fall within the tent of "queer Black mothering" by virtue of their class, care responsibilities, gender nonconformity, and/or transness, and yet hate the work, desire something else, and simply do not find themselves in the romance. We must stay vigilant in asking: when does the "queer" pose no challenge to property? To what *end* are we queering motherhood? To what end (King dares us to ask) redeeming and uplifting the queer figure of the Black Matriarch? What would happen to our politics, were she not redeemed? I take King's point to be that valorizing Black mother-ers simply on the terms of "motherhood" risks foreclosing other possible forms of identity and sidelining subjects who might not be all that interested in redemption anyway. The question is, are we willing to countenance a *destructive* queer Black female subject, rather than a merely productive one? If so, what non-redemptive pathways might we help blaze, in more interesting directions— collective subject-positions after the family, and beyond motherhood?

Ten years after "Mama's Baby, Papa's Maybe," the British feminist critical race theorist Hazel Carby published a very different landmark intervention entitled "White Woman Listen!" Whereas Spillers had judged the family as potentially beyond redemption, Carby's target was, instead, the women's movement's rigid antipathy to the family. Most Black feminists "would not wish to deny that the family can be a source of oppression for us," she wrote; yet many still felt frustrated at white feminists' overemphasis on it as a site of oppression. "The black family has been a site of political and cultural resistance to racism," Carby stressed.[7] It's true, of course. There can be no family-abolitionism without an appreciation for everything the family affords by way of *resistant* ethnic and communitarian identity, pleasure, and (above all) survival. We must face the question: whose family are we abolishing? Still, the answer may not be what we expect.

The answer might be, in fact: *my family first, please*! Tiffany Lethabo King, for example, writes of her "commitment to the ongoing life of the Black intramural" (Black internal/indoor life) as it is lived within her "own extended Black diasporic family":

> While I exist blissfully and sometimes uneasily within a formation that must constantly be reshaped—and eventually even abolished—in order to be capacious and loving enough to address its own violence and continue to invite in all of those that desire its embrace, it may be necessary to go "beyond" it. While I critique the family and am committed to addressing its limitations—even its elimination—I celebrate the creative ways that Black descendants of captive communities continue to reinvent and conceptualize relationships. To this Black endeavor, I will always be committed.[8]

Manifestly, then, it is possible to love one's Black family while grasping that the family emerged historically as a category of "violent forms of humanism."[9] In fact, it is probably *because* of such love that one might wish to fight, like Tiffany, against the family-form: that "site of violence and dehumanization that threatens to engulf Black sociality."[10]

The debate between family "reform" or "expansion" and family abolition is "not a mere semantic quibble," then, as Barrett and McIntosh observed in 1982. I agree with them: while we might not have all the answers right away, ultimately, "it will be important to determine whether the positive ideals and satisfactions that we hope to strengthen spring *from* the family or—as we shall argue—survive in spite of it."[11]

All of this is maximally difficult political terrain. If the family is a combined-and-uneven form of thriving, denied to some, while being a combined-and-uneven mechanism of violence, concentrating power in the hands of others, it is foolish to imagine that there is an interpellative strategy we could "safely" choose that would also be adequate to the magnitude of the problem that is the family. One option is to specify, when we talk about abolition of the family, that we mean the white, cisheteropatriarchal, nuclear, colonial family. This might feel safer, but might actually pose more dangers in its invitation to excuse or romanticize the political character of all nonwhite, mixed, gay, and/or indigenous homes, while neglecting most people's family-abolitionist needs and excluding them from family abolitionist politics!

Another option is to cleave to the infinitely harder line and say that for historical reasons no other family than this family exists—*the* family. Obviously, nonwhite households represent a planetary majority. Many families aren't straight, nor even cis-sexual, nor part of a program of colonizing settlement. But while whiteness, empire, and heterosex have lots to do with the family, the family's most fundamental feature, as Kathi Weeks insists,[12] is that it privatizes care: a process of enclosure in which all kinds of families unintentionally participate. So, if we plump for the second option, then the family is to be abolished even when it is aspired to, mythologized, valued, and embodied by people who are neither white nor heterosexual, neither bourgeois nor colonizers. And this latter position, as you can see, is the position I believe to be correct. While there is no equality or justice in the distribution of "kinfulness" between humans on this Earth, and while there is no sense in which white, straight and/or bourgeois people *deserve* to reap the rewards of everybody else's courage in abolishing the family, it is yet only in collectively letting go of this technology of privatization, the family, that our species will truly prosper.

At present, it is standard among practically all communities to fête the family as a bastion of relative safety from state persecution and market coercion, and as a space for nurturing subordinated cultural practices, languages, and traditions. But this is not enough of a reason to spare the family. Frustratedly, Hazel Carby stressed the fact (for the benefit of her white sisters) that many racially, economically, and patriarchally oppressed people cleave proudly and fervently to the family. She was right; nevertheless, as Kathi Weeks puts it: "the model of the nuclear family that has served subordinated groups as a fence against the state, society and capital *is the very same* white, settler, bourgeois, heterosexual, and patriarchal institution that was imposed by the state, society, and capital on the formerly enslaved, indigenous peoples, and waves of immigrants, all of whom continue to be at once in need of its meagre protections and marginalized by its legacies and prescriptions" (emphasis mine).[13] The family is a shield that human beings have taken up, quite rightly, to survive a war. If we cannot countenance ever putting down that shield, perhaps we have forgotten that the war does not have to go on forever.

This is why Paul Gilroy remarked in his 1993 essay "It's A Family Affair," "even the best of this discourse of the familialization of politics is still a problem."[14] Gilroy is grappling with the reality that, in the United Kingdom as in the United States, the state's constant disrespect of the Black home and transgression of Black households' boundaries, as well as its disproportionate removal of Black children into the foster-care industry, understandably inspires an urgent anti-racist politics of "familialization" in defense of Black families. Both the British and American netherworlds of supposedly "broken" homes (milieus that are then exoticized, and seen as efflorescing creatively against all odds), have posed an obstinate threat to the legitimacy of the family regime simply by existing, Gilroy suggests. The paradox is that the "broken" remnant *sustains* the bourgeois regime insofar as it supplies the culture, inspiration, and oftentimes the surrogate care labor that allows the white household to imagine itself as whole. As a dialectician, "I want to have it both ways," writes Gilroy, closing out his essay. "I want to be able to valorize what we can recover, but also to cite the disastrous consequences that follow when the family supplies the only symbols of political agency we can find in the culture and the only object upon which that agency can be seen to operate. Let us remind ourselves that there are other possibilities."[15]

There are other possibilities! Traces of the desire for them can be found in Toni Cade (later Toni Cade Bambara)'s anthology *The Black Woman*, published in America in 1970, not long after the publication of the US labor secretariat's "Moynihan report," *The Negro Family: The Case for National Action*. The open season on the Black Matriarch was in full swing. And certainly not all of the anthology's feminists, in their valiant effort to beat back societal anti-maternal sentiment (matropho-bia) and the hatred of Black women specifically (more recently known as "misogynoir"), make the additional step of criticizing familism within their Black communities. But one or two contributors do flatly reject the notion that the family could ever be a part of Black (collective human) liberation. Kay Lindsey, in her piece "The Black Woman as a Woman," lays out her analysis that: "If all white institutions with the exception of the family were destroyed, the state could also rise again, but Black rather than white."[16] In other words: the only way to ensure the destruction of the patriarchal state is for the institution of the family to be destroyed. "And I mean destroyed," echoes the feminist women's health center representative Pat Parker in 1980, in a speech she delivered at ¡Basta! Women's Conference on Imperialism and Third World War in Oakland, California. Parker speaks in the name of The Black Women's Revolutionary Council, among other organizations, and her wide-ranging statement (which addresses imperialism, the Klan, and movement-building) purposively ends with the family: "As long as women are bound by the nuclear family structure we cannot effectively move toward revolution. And if women don't move, it will not happen."[17] The left, along with women especially of the upper and middle classes, "must give up . . . undying loyalty to the nuclear family," Parker charges. It is "the basic unit of capitalism and in order for us to move to revolution it has to be destroyed."

Forty years later, the British writer Lola Olufemi is among those reminding us that there are other possibilities: "abolishing the family . . ." she tweets, "that's light work. You're crying over whether or not Engels said it when it's been focal to black studies/black feminism for decades."[18] For Olufemi as for Parker and Lindsey, abolishing marriage, private property, white supremacy, and capitalism are projects that cannot be disentangled from one another. She is no lone voice, either. Annie Olaloku-Teriba, a British scholar of "Blackness" in theory and history, is another contemporary exponent of the rich Black family-abolitionist tradition Olufemi names. In 2021, Olaloku-Teriba surprised and unsettled some of her followers by publishing a thread animated by a commitment to the overthrow of "familial relations"[19] as a key goal of her antipatriarchal socialism. These posts point to the striking absence of the child from contemporary theorizations of patriarchal domesticity, and criticize radicals' reluctance to call mothers who "violently discipline [Black] boys into masculinity" *patriarchal.* "The adult/child relation is as central to patriarchy as 'man'/'woman,'" Olaloku-Teriba affirms: "The domination of the boy by the woman is a very routine and potent expression of patriarchal power." These observations reopen horizons. What would it mean for Black caregivers (of all genders) not to fear the absence of family in the lives of Black children? What would it mean not to *need* the Black family?

In the next chapter, we will race through the complex, dual-strand history of family abolitionism (in some cases, the movements avowed themselves as such; in others, they have been glossed that way by me). On the one hand, we'll see, people dreamed of erotic town planning, kitchenless architecture, nationalized childcare, ectogenesis, children's political emancipation, gay liberation, posthousework pleasures, and radical welfare activism. On the other, people were stealing away, refusing to breed, birthing in secrecy, eluding marriage, maintaining ties, remembering ancestors, and springing people free. On the one hand, there was an uneven, disorganized movement, from within the matrix of state-sanctioned kinship, seeking to burst free of its confines by mounting experiments in counter-social reproduction: women's strikes, lesbians' custody battles, free schools, communes, men's childcare collectives. On the other hand, in parallel, people arrived at ways of being—forms of maroon (fugitive ex-slave) togetherness that have sometimes also been called "the undercommons"[20]—capable of surviving successive attempts to impose the familial property regime.

3

A Potted History of Family Abolitionism

"We are already outside the family."
—Gay Liberation Front Manifesto[1]

Family abolitionism has by no means been a continuous or even consciously coalitional campaign, but people have been arguing for—and sometimes building—alternatives to the family for two thousand years at least. In Book V of *The Republic*, Socrates concludes that the family must be abolished because, well, it is obviously unfair. (In the dry formula of one contemporary political philosopher, "families disrupt fair patterns of distribution and, in particular, equality of opportunity."[2]) Whether to abolish the family or preserve it is thus not just an essay question on Plato to be assigned to sophomores. It is one of the most strictly classical debates in philosophy, pursued earnestly in juridical journals to this day.[3]

Abstract philosophizing has not been the whole story, however. Over the course of the last two centuries, militants and radicals of various kinds have been manifesting—and writing manifestos about—experimentally abolishing the family from northern France, to occupied

Palestine, to settler-colonized Chicago. What follows is a necessarily non-comprehensive whistle-stop tour, not of legal position papers, but of lived and struggled-for versions and visions of family abolition, focusing on Europe and the US.

Charles Fourier

Besides inventing the word "feminism," the French silk merchant Charles Fourier is the reason "utopia" is often associated with seas of lemonade (an early climate ecologist and geoengineer, he really predicted these). More to the point, Fourier identified the single-family dwelling as one of the chief obstacles to improving the position of women in the world. This fundamental insight inspired an international movement of utopic land projects, including some that sought to abolish the woman-crushing norm of the private kitchen in favor of so-called "kitchenless" cities—neighborhoods furnished with open common kitchens and superb free canteens.[4] Unquestionably sensible as this was, many of Fourier's ideas were unusual: for instance, he opposed bread (being in favor of pastry) as well as the number ten; and expected that sharks and lions would be evolutionarily replaced by "anti-sharks" and "anti-lions." As Dominic Pettman explains, he had a complicated physical account of how "we live in the worst of possible worlds, but are only a few months away from flipping this scenario on its head."[5]

Fourier clearly got a lot wrong—and was moreover a racist colonialist who wasn't at all sure about abolishing wealth inequality. But he also developed powerful theories of human alienation and of repression many years before Marx and Freud. By attacking the family as the cornerstone of market domination and "civilization," he has helped countless people to recognize, in the words of one biographer, "the contradictions, the wasted opportunities and the hidden possibilities of our own lives."[6] Starting in the 1840s, the Fourierist movement founded intentional communities throughout America and Europe based on his polyamorous, anti-work visions.[7] By some measures—given that all these communes petered out, succumbed to state repression, or imploded nastily—Fourierism clearly failed. By other measures, one might say it's too early to tell.

Born into the petty bourgeoisie in the north of France, Fourier was about eighteen years old at the time of the French Revolution. Electrified by the momentum of history, he abandoned his plans to become an architectural engineer and dedicated himself instead to writing, one might say, an architecture of the future. He wrote at night while continuing to be a tradesman by day, and came to hate intensely everything he called "civilized" (meaning, primarily, work, and bourgeois culture, that is, hypocrisy, private property, and markets). By the time he died in his sixties, he had published several tracts—notably *The New Amorous World* and *The Theory of the Four Movements*—laying out elaborate designs, right down to the last meticulous detail, for a post-capitalist human society whose essential features remain pretty convincing to many people today. What exactly did he prescribe? Among other things: universal basic income, escape from markets, nonmonogamy, excellent food, and varied recreation for all generations. All living is communal (in vast buildings called "phalanxes" or "phalansteries," numbering 1,600 people).[8] There are covered walkways for when the weather is bad, and a guaranteed sexual pleasure minimum. All labor is fully deprivatized (tasks are shared among all children and adults, as well as organized according to the human personality's established "Laws of Passionate Attraction"). Work thus transmogrifies into a libidinal art, or joyful play. Regular carefully curated sex parties are presided over by special "Fairies."

Fourier's obsessive notes constitute the first known detailed blueprint for a European utopia. The utopia in question, to quote McKenzie Wark, is "an amorous order for women, the elderly and perverts," advanced via a kind of "systems theory porn"[9] that anticipates Paul Preciado's pharmacopornographic account of capitalism. Fourier dubbed this world-to-come "Harmony," and an inordinate amount of calculation and tabulation was involved in programming the blend of spicy discord and sweet compatibility that science showed was key to Harmonian happiness. Alas, Fourier's forte was not political economy, but his analyses of gender, ecology, bourgeois morality, and marriage were rightly taken seriously by dissidents throughout the nineteenth and twentieth centuries—from Owen, Bebel, Marx, Engels, Kropotkin, and Lenin to Walter Benjamin, André Breton, David Harvey, and contemporary sex radicals like Wark and O'Brien. "His spirit," it has been said, "entered the conceptual groundwater."[10] Most impressively, Fourier understood that men "even debase the female sex by their flattery of it."[11] Fully committed to female sexual freedom, he promulgated an orgiastic proto-queer theory *avant la lettre*. The original feminism, then, is inseparable from family abolition, queer sex, and socialist utopian-ism. Good to know, right? *Vive le phalanstère!*

The Queer Indigenous and Maroon Nineteenth Century

It is vital at this point to note that pre-colonized and Indigenous populations—for instance in Africa and North America—by and large did not develop the form of private property "the family." Rather, they had it imposed on them as part of the process of disciplining them into capitalism.[12] And while assimilated modes of life have certainly taken significant hold among First Nations throughout the Americas (a function of the ongoing catastrophe that has been the past four hundred years, from their perspective), familialization is also an ongoing, not just "historic," process of colonization. As "The Critical Polyamorist"—Sisseton Wahpeton Oyate scholar Kim TallBear—says of the Indigenous experience: "colo-nial notions of family insidiously continue to stigmatize us as they represent the normative standard against which we are measured."[13] For example, eighteenth-century British colonists endeavored explicitly to destroy the systems of sex equality, involving female political power ("petticoat government,"[14] in their eyes), operative among Native peoples such as the Cherokee. In the nineteenth century, the US and Canadian federal governments' Indian policies typically demanded marriage as a way of dissolving tribal models of collective ownership that went along with gender-nonbinarism, non-monogamy, and/or matrilocal open marriage: they instituted private property and then concentrated it in the hands of "heads of house-hold," that is, husbands.[15] It is in this sense that we can say that family abolition—as a project of resistance to and flight from bourgeois society and a *defense* against colonization—was a horizon raised via the practices of stolen, captive, colonially displaced, and/or formerly enslaved people who defied the institutions and modes of citizenship the US attempted to acculturate them to, namely: private property, secularized Christian monogamy, and the marriage-based private nuclear household.

A couple of hours' drive west of my Philadelphia home—in Carlisle, Pennsylvania—a so-called "Indian Cemetery" contains the bones of two hundred very young Indigenous prisoners-of-war: children whom US settler-colonists stole from their people and imprisoned in the Carlisle Indian Industrial School (1879–1918). At Carlisle, the Native children were educated by civilizers, anthropologists, and gentle maternalist genocidaires like Alice C. Fletcher, who inculcated what TallBear has called "settler sexuality." Between 1879–1900, the Bureau of Indian Affairs opened twenty-four such off-reservation schools, by the end of which time three-quarters of all Native children had been enrolled in boarding schools, on- or off-reservation. Army memos from the period show that holding the tribes' youngest members hostage in this manner was an explicit bid to dissuade adult Native warriors from mounting armed counter-offensives ("make them behave themselves") as well as a method of imposing "the" family by breaking kinship ties. Shifting attention away from direct slaughter to the destruction of tribal relationships and ways-of-being, the American government's Indian Schools policy marked a transitional moment in the settler-colonial process, the passage from the military maxim "The only good Indian is a dead Indian" to the new, reform-minded motto of

Carlisle's founder, Richard Henry Pratt, aimed at remaking human identity in the oedipal grid: "Kill the Indian, save the man." Attempts—by kin and living ancestors of the stolen children—to claim them back, to contest new genocidal legislation, to raise consciousness about the schools as academies of death, and later to ensure the young ones' proper burial and remembrance, have not ceased since 1879.

Some Indigenous diplomats and philosophers became great enforcers of Christian morality and patriarchy (such as the Seneca leader Handsome Lake, who precipitated what has been called "the Iroquois's own version of Salem" in 1803, for example).[16] However, especially before colonization—and sometimes continuously, into the present—most Native tribes practiced few or no forms of patriarchy; raising children collectively, honoring more than two genders, placing only loose social strictures on sexual pleasure, counting nonhuman relatives among their kin, and sometimes conceptualizing mothering-practices (such as breast-feeding) as gender-inclusive and diplomatically important.[17] Indigenous American two-spirit gender subjectivity, Indigenous philosophical traditions, and Indigenous cultures of sexual freedom have inspired and educated gender-dissident settlers for four centuries; in the sixties and seventies, entire communities of Gay Liberationists sought to emulate "queer" indigeneity. "There have been glimmers of interconnectivity across Indigenous life and gay practice," summarizes the Navajo writer Lou Cornum, in "Desiring the Tribe," a 2019 essay about the history of utopianist gay and lesbian interactions with (and appropriations of) Native practices. Refusing to simply condemn what is "cringey" (in their own words) about these glimmers, Cornum sees promise in them, and wonders if "a lens as large as communist thinking might direct this wavering light forward" in the twenty-first century.[18] With Cornum, my hope is that non-indigenous and Indigenous communists today could move together toward some kind of collective reckoning with this legacy of kinship-erasure and -reinvention, and develop a shared language of *abolition of the family as a decolonial imperative*.

People newly emancipated from chattel slavery in the US also pursued heterogeneous, anti-propertarian versions of kinship. Before the Civil War, a diversity of covert romantic and sexual codes—including nonmonogamous and loose marriages dedicated to the care of "sweetheart children"—developed among the captive laborers who had been stolen (or birthed by those stolen) from their African communities, and transported over the Atlantic via the Middle Passage.[19] Slavers systematically raped slaves (adulterously) and impregnated them (concubinage) even as they were supposedly modeling the human—that is, white—values of frugality, hard work, and lifelong, monogamous, biologically fruitful marriage, oriented toward heritable property accumulation, as master pioneers of the New World. Meanwhile, for the people they had artificially rendered "kinless," sometimes it was desirable to practice forms of counter-familiality, solidarity, and connection (*family is as family does*) among themselves: mothering young people who happened to be in the same slaver's household; making and revising claims about biological paternity, as needed; "returning" a wife or a husband to their former wife or husband when circumstances permitted, and so on. Customs such as these laid the ground for an ongoing tradition of Black non-nuclear kinning and "polymaternalism" that scholars from Cathy Cohen to Alexis Pauline Gumbs have described as structurally queer.[20]

Mothering outside of motherhood—and outside even of *womanhood* as it was defined in white supremacist law and science—became a collective art which, while born of necessity and survival, nevertheless consciously manifested abolitionist desire and alternative visions of social reproduction. This is not to romanticize: sometimes comradely mothering in the context of slavery meant brutalizing, heartbreaking refusals to reproduce enslaved life. Pregnant Caribbean captives, for instance, found secret herbalist ways to stop manufacturing new human commodities, or to extinguish them once they were born.[21] More generally, trafficked humans, young and old, were compelled to adapt their commitments to one another to surviving long periods of sudden separation. Nurturing relations was thus a form of *marronage* (stealing-away, forming maroon communities)—a stealing-away of the captive person's kinful, related self. Unsurprisingly, then, after Reconstruction, freedmen, -women, and children did not on the whole jump headfirst into the family.

Historians have found that newly emancipated Americans still maintained "diversity of relationship and family structures greater than their white contemporaries on farms or in factories."[22] That is, from the state's point of view, too many freedpeople still tended to cohabit promiscuously, raise children non-monogamously, and take an alarmingly relaxed approach to the meaning of marriage. It was this worrying "failure" of the freed population to seek access to the wages of private familiality that prompted a raft of social workers, church ministers, police, and lawmakers to aggressively mandate legal marriage and to begin prosecutions of African American "violations" of marital decency.[23] These same actors had previously been unsure whether they even wanted to instate a marital Black family (or for that matter an indigenous, Latino, or Chinese one), on account of their concern that this might interfere with eugenic nation-building. But the American state's policing of the post-Reconstruction Black marital bed laid the basis for twentieth-century welfare officers' "man-in-the-house" rule, which denied benefits to any mother caught "living" (even just for a couple of hours) with a member of the opposite sex.[24] If you, a Black woman, had a "man in the house" of any kind, the law declared, then that man, not the state, ought to be the one paying your child support.

Those who have dug critically into the archives of anti-slavery caregiving, loving, and sexual or gender self-expression have tended to find a willfully deviant profusion of anti-genealogical fugitivities: all kinds of ways of negating, pre-dating, ignoring, and/or provincializing the private nuclear household. Beginning in the late nineteenth century, in *Wayward Lives, Beautiful Experiments: Intimate Histories of Riotous Black Girls, Troublesome Women, and Queer Radicals*,[25] Saidiya Hartman documents criminalized "unwed mothers raising children; same-sex households; female breadwinners; families composed of siblings, aunts, and children," sex workers, prison-saboteurs, bulldykes, and more. Hartman resists, however, the urge to romanticize the unruly lives of the punished, constrained, and oppressed turn-of-the-century women who interest her, even while calling their experiments in refusing respectability *beautiful*. For her, "the generosity and mutuality of the poor" shines forth from all these various manifestations of what I want to call family-abolitionism-from-below. "Here is the abolition of the working-class family without its naturalized rein-scription," comments M. E. O'Brien appreciatively, about a similar archive.[26]

The Era of the Communist Manifesto

Family abolitionism is, despite what some socialists say, orthodox Marxism. According to the hallowed fathers of proletarian revolution, communism calls for the "aboli-tion of all rights of inheritance." Indeed, unlike several of the revolutionary philosophers of their time—notably the anarchists Proudhon and Bakunin—the nineteenth-century Germans Karl Marx and Friedrich Engels were completely opposed to the family by 1844. As we have seen, they were hardly the instigators of the politics. Besides Fourier, in France, "libertarian" communists like Joseph Déjacque, in France, believed in "Abolition of the family, the family based on marriage, the authority of father and spouse . . . The liberation of woman, the eman-cipation of the child."[27] Meanwhile, in Manchester, England, and Lanark, Scotland, the Welsh socialist and philanthropist Robert Owen was promulgating family-abolitionism on a "cooperative," group-marriage based model.[28] Sharing the weakness of these other analyses, unfortunately, Marx and Engels's gradual arrival at their anti-family position was not informed by thinking about slavery's simultaneous destruction of the family and imposition of it on its victims. Rather, it was explicitly indebted to (among other things) Marx's time spent in Paris and exposure to Fourier.[29]

Marx and Engels were greatly critical of Fourier's (and all utopian socialists' and anarchists') overall project. Nevertheless, the very first footnote to *The German Ideology* states the following: "That the abolition of individual economy is inseparable from the abolition of the family, is self-evident."[30] Despite being so self-evident, family abolition was included in the Communist Manifesto: it is, famously, the "infamous proposal of the Communists" that makes "even the most radical flare up."[31] This passage is where Marx and Engels deride "bourgeois claptrap about the family and education (*Erziehung*) . . . the hallowed co-relation of parent and child"; and where they state that the ruling class has "reduced the family to a mere money relation" and "torn away the sentimental veil" that once shrouded it. A common misreading of this passage insists that Marx and Engels would like to reverse the process of "reduction" and "unveiling." In this view, the authors are only noting that capitalism has already basically abolished the family; and they are actually *defending* themselves against the false accusation that they want to finish the job!

In reality, it wasn't only the families of the bourgeoisie that Marx and Engels wanted to abolish. They did consider it gruesome that capital accumulation so relentlessly undermined, degraded, and fragmented proletarian kinship. Nevertheless, they explained, the male-breadwinner family *aspired to* by large sections of the working class was irreducibly bourgeois in form. It was one of three interrelated enemies of Communism the two friends referred to as "the Parties of Order," namely: Religion, Family, and the State. They even chided their comrade Hermann Kriege for failing to advocate elimination of the family. In his *Economic and Philosophic Manuscripts*, Marx reflected movingly that the "positive supersession (*Aufhebung*) of private property" would necessarily "return" people "out of religion, family, state, etc."—returning us to our proper, "human, i.e., social existence."

For Marx, our collective "return" to our human, i.e., social existence is, at the same time, a transcendence of nature and an exit from the institutions of order. He isn't saying that the family is natural (and natural = bad), nor is he saying that there's nothing natural about the family (and unnatural = bad). Rather, he's saying that there's nothing immutably *natural or unnatural* about *us*. Marx's and Engels' position—which is far more attuned to the "dialectical" relationship of nature and culture, in this respect, than Fourier's—was "a decisive move away from the naturalism of their predecessors," according to Richard Weikart. In a communist society, "even if people had a natural bond to their children, no provision would be made for this . . . No compulsion would interfere with relationships. Thus, theoretically, any sexual relationship between mutually consenting persons would be possible. What would *not* be possible would be the security of a life-long marriage. This sexual relationship could not be chosen."[32]

To achieve this postfamilial communist society, the Communist Manifesto proposes to "replace home education by social." For some contemporary Marxists—notably Jules Joanne Gleeson and Kate Doyle Griffiths in their 2015 text "Kinderkommunismus: A Feminist Analysis of the 21st Century Family and a Communist Proposal for its Abolition"—the means to implement this social education is necessarily "coercive" even if one of its central purposes is to "destroy coercion." The institution that is required, in these authors' view, is a compulsory transgenerational revolutionary crèche: "There is no such thing as a libertarian upbringing. At present, children are taught to feel desperation and to accommodate themselves to capitalism by parents and other care workers living under capitalist conditions. The crèche would be a communist institution, driving children instead to forge themselves into the face of a new society."[33] For others—in this case, China Miéville— "Advocating social education, rather than privatized and familial education, is not to propose indoctrination, but countering the doctrines of the ruling class."[34] I sympathize with both positions. I wonder if, in the era of the Communist Manifesto—when socialist texts met with a non-negligible audience—we might posit that a popular appetite existed for a certain kind of collective *self*-indoctrination: a desire to be remade entirely as a self, outside of the bourgeois family story.

Alexandra Kollontai and Early Bolshevik Utopianism

In her 1920 pamphlet "Communism and the Family," the Soviet family abolitionist Alexandra Kollontai fleshes out Marx and Engels's horizon of post-familial life: "society will gradually take upon itself all the tasks that before the revolution fell to the individual parents." The obligations of parents to their children shall "wither away gradually," she reasons hopefully, "until finally society assumes the full responsibility."[35] Empathetically and repeatedly, Kollontai reassures her readers that they have "no need to be alarmed":

Communist society takes care of every child and guarantees both him and his mother material and moral support. Society will feed, bring up and educate the child. At the same time, those parents who desire to participate in the education of their children will by no means be prevented from doing so. Communist society will take upon itself all the duties involved ... but the joys of parenthood will not be taken away from those who are capable of appreciating them. Such are the plans of communist society and they can hardly be interpreted as the forcible destruction of the family and the forcible separation of child from mother.

Kollontai is, however, demanding something magnificent from the "working women" addressed here. "The narrow and exclusive affection of the mother for her own children must expand," she declares, "until it extends to all the children of the great, proletarian family." Kollontai, in sum, envisions a planetary insurgency of *red love*, "a social love: a love of many in many ways."[36]

Comrade Alexandra was born into a liberal aristocratic household in St. Petersburg in 1872 but was helping organize textile workers strikes by her early twenties.[37] In order to escape her family, she married a gentleman called Kollontai in 1893. Five years later, she left him and their child to study Marxism in Zurich (where women were allowed to study), becoming an expert on the Finnish class struggle. In 1908, Alexandra began her first period of exile from Russia because the Tsarist government had issued a warrant for her arrest, following a decade of her propagandizing for international—particularly women's—labor revolution with her faction of the Social Democratic Labour Party. She campaigned against WWI throughout Europe. In 1915, she even toured the United States. Kollontai, albeit a feminist by any reasonable standard, always made it clear that she did not consider herself a feminist because the word "feminist," in her milieu, signified classed self-interest on the part of ladies (that is, mere bourgeois-individualist suffragism). In her pamphlets "The Social Basis of the Women's Question" and "Love and the New Morality," she theorized the family as a labor division, and sexuality as a comradely matter—a concept later articulated as "winged Eros." In her "Letter to Working Youth" on this proposed new erotic ideal, she denounced the couple-form: "Bourgeois morality demanded all for the loved one. The morality of the proletariat demands all for the collective."[38]

The February 1917 overthrow of the Tsar enabled her to return to Russia and—who knows!— contribute to an erotic revolution and the positive supersession of the family. Having joined the Bolsheviks, Kollontai helped strategize, on the party's central committee, toward the October uprising. She helped, thereafter, draft a law on marriage, which allowed women to get divorce on demand, even without the husband's permission, and to receive alimony. Aged forty-five, divorced, and at the helm of a possible planetary metamorphosis, she briefly went AWOL before turning up married to a sailor seventeen years her junior (Pavel Dybenko, who was executed under Stalin in 1938). A powerhouse, polyglot, and philosopher, she wrote many wonderful speeches on the subjects of sex, love, war, child welfare, parenthood, and the nexus of gender and class. She traveled constantly to myriad congresses while also writing propaganda novels about the complicated psychology of the sexual "New Woman" (*Red Love, Great Love, The Love of Worker Bees*). Notably, her hope for human sexuality was expressed via the "glass of water" theory: the hypothesis that sex would come to be as abundant and necessary to everyone in society's eyes—but also as *unremarkable*—as drinking a glass of water.

As chronicled in the legendary title *Autobiography of a Sexually Emancipated Communist Woman* (1926), party support for her agenda of liberating sex from reproduction, equalizing men and women's pay, setting up free crèches, and abolishing the family was very lacking: in particular, "my efforts to nationalize maternity and infant care set off . . . insane attacks against me."[39] Nevertheless, for a brief moment, Kollontai managed to force the politics of proletarian reproductive liberation—espoused too by figures like Inessa Armand and Clara Zetkin—onto Lenin's desk. For a brief moment, after all—before she resigned in left-communist protest of her comrades' ratification of the Brest-Litovsk treaty, which ceded Finland to the whites—Alexandra was the People's Commissar for Social Welfare in the first Soviet government. Her most celebrated accomplishment was her founding, in 1918, with Armand, of the Zhenotdel—the women's department of the Party—which legalized abortion but also, wrongheadedly, sought to liberate Muslim women from their burqas.

Unlike Fourier and unlike Marx (but like most Marxists of her day), Kollontai considered work to be the key to liberation, and the worker the subject of post-capitalism. Work, work, and more (revolutionary) work ought to have occupied the bulk of her own female life, she lamented in her autobiography—instead of all that pointless bloody love. Productive labors, not caring ones, ought to be the life's mission of women, in Kollontai's view. Socializing care is a sine qua non of socialism; but this is because, for Kollontai, work, not care, is what ultimately makes history.

In 1921–22, Alexandra stood with the anti-authoritarian Worker's Opposition, a dissenting faction internal to the Party, and courageously signed the so-called Letter of the Twenty-Two (which likewise sought to resist the entrenchment of a despotic leadership). Thus, by the mid-1920s, she was exiled from her country once again—this time, under the guise of decades-long diplomatic postings overseas, including a substantial stint in Mexico—by the revolutionary USSR she had helped create. Tragically, Alexandra Kollontai seems to have abandoned her liberationist, syndicalist beliefs, serving Stalin from afar for the rest of her life, even as he reinstated the most anti-communist (not to mention gender-conservative and patriarchal) forms of social order. She never criticized Stalin publicly, survived, and died in Russia in 1952. There is no ignoring her capitulations, yet one can still derive, I feel, considerable pleasure from the fact that for several decades, the best-known ambassador for the USSR around the world was not just *one of the first women ever to hold diplomatic office* (a fact that never seems to come up in histories of the girlboss) but a glamorous high femme libertine and family abolitionist. Even as Kollontai's "red love" imagination failed to question sufficiently the edifice of wage labor and its compatibility with a free human future, her prole sexual liberation politics and "debauched" personal mores inspired millions of human beings around the world, and continue to do so to this day. They may have made her the subject of frenzied smears throughout the media as well as, shamefully, her own party, but, one hundred years later, her name is held in honor among sex-positive reds everywhere.

Red Love: A Reader on Alexandra Kollontai is a giant tome of neo-Kollontaian manifestos, letters, struggle bulletins, interviews, plays, and essays, published in 2020 in Berlin.[40] That same year, the Spanish artist Dora García published *Love With Obstacles* (or in the original: *Amor Rojo*), a textual compendium of all her collaborative research on Kollontai's life and legacy, to accompany her film of the same name.[41] I encountered García's "red love" archive and film-making in the context of her 2022 Kollontai-themed exhibition in Brooklyn ("*Revolution, Fulfill Your Promise!*"), towards which I contributed workshops alongside the trans revolutionary M. E. O'Brien. The links García draws between the Bolshevik's family-abolitionism, contemporary Mexican transfeminisms, and abortion-defense street militancy moved me to tears.[42] We will never know, all these anthologies and moving images suggest, what Kollontai might have accomplished with her comrades on Russia's domestic front in terms of the transformation of bourgeois love into "winged eros" and "love-comradeship," had the counterrevolution not prevailed. For it bears repeating that Kollontai's family abolitionism was actively thwarted by other Bolsheviks. Michael Hardt narrates:

> For the 8th Party Congress in 1919, Kollontai prepared an amendment to affirm in explicit terms the withering away of the family, but Lenin, although sympathetic to her aims, claimed that it was not yet the right time: "we have in fact," he is reported to have responded, "to save the family."[43]

Shulamith Firestone, Revolutionary Feminism, and the Limits of the Kibbutz

Saving the family has been the mission of a huge number of history's feminists—which is partly why Kollontai (who, again, did not even see herself as a feminist) often opposed movements calling themselves feminisms. But it's time now to skip over almost fifty years, moving from Leningrad to the Lower East Side, and meet the Jewish New Yorker, Chicago art-school graduate, and messianic feminist Shulamith Firestone, whose hilarious and readable yet densely philosophical Freudian-Reichian-Marxist-Engelsian-Beauvoirian manifesto for family abolition (published in 1970) she composed at the advanced age of twenty-four.[44]

While, oddly, this manifesto never mentions Kollontai by name, its author does suggest—alas, without elaborating—that "The failure of the Russian Revolution is directly traceable to the failure of its attempts to eliminate the family and sexual repression."[45] Hungry for clues as to how better to restart the attempts, Shulie Firestone traveled to Israel to study life on a settler-socialist kibbutz, pored over Philippe Ariès's controversial history of the invention of the child, *Centuries of Childhood* (trans. 1962), and scrutinized the international "free schooling" or "unschooling" movement more generally, especially the "radical approach to childrearing" enacted by A. S. Neill in his fee-paying pseudo-commune for children, Summerhill, in Suffolk, England.[46] Disappointed by her experiences, she reported back to her American sisters that the "far left" kibbutzniks were almost exactly as sexually conservative and patriarchal as their non-left counterparts and, indeed, wider society. All in all, she said, "the kibbutz is nothing more than a community of farming pioneers temporarily forced to sacrifice traditional social structures to better adjust to a peculiar set of national conditions."[47]

The self-appointed founder and theorist of the American women's liberation movement, Firestone advocated for "the abolition of the labor force itself under a cybernetic socialism" and "the diffusion of the childbearing and childrearing role to the society as a whole, men as well as women." Ectogenesis—the machine uterus—is notoriously a part of this speculative picture.[48] But above all, she contends, women must liberate children and themselves from the capitalist patriarchy—seizing control over technology, eradicating the tyranny of work, automating labor (even reproductive labor, as far as possible), and shedding the incest taboo such that play, love, and sexuality might "[flow] unimpeded."[49] This is why the stakes of the (unsurprising) failure of kibbutzim to abolish the family on occupied Palestinian land could not have been higher for many US women in 1970. As Kathi Weeks affirms in the opening of her wittily titled essay "The Most Infamous Feminist Proposal," the "infamous proposal of the communists" briefly became the position of the women's liberation movement.

Yes, women's liberation, at its fiery peak, meant: abolishing the family. In 1969, Linda Gordon's extended statement "Functions of the Family" appeared in the self-published US movement mimeograph *WOMEN: A Journal of Liberation*, outlining the revolutionary-feminist position that "the nuclear family must be destroyed, and people must find better ways of living together. Furthermore, this process must precede as well as follow the overthrow of capitalism."[50] It was the following year that the mainstream publication of *The Dialectic of Sex: The Case for Feminist Revolution* shook the world. Firestone's magnum opus voices scalding refusals of almost every "natural" premise of American society ("almost," because its chapter on race is woefully racist; and because no queer people appear in it).[51] It advances a vision of a future in which children and adults together—having eliminated capitalism, work, and the sex distinction itself—democratically inhabit large, nongenetic households. You see, Shulie deemed the overthrowing of class, work, and markets to be a self-evidently necessary task, barely worth defending. What really interested her was the abolition of culture and nature, no less: starting with patriarchal "love" and its "culture of romance" on the one hand, and pregnancy on the other.

The scale of Shulie's ambition was startling to readers. But in 1970 readers at least had some contexts for her proposal to abolish the sex and generational distinctions. At that time, practically all feminists, from Kate Millett to Toni Cade Bambara, were condemning the family as oppressive to women and children, anti-erotic, and/or white supremacist.[52] "Patriarchy's chief institution is the family," Millett wrote in 1968.[53] Even Betty Friedan, before recanting her anti-family positions a decade later, called the private home "a comfortable concentration camp" in 1963. Free universal 24/7 community-run child-care was a *middle-of-the-road* feminist demand. If today many of us don't know this history of the women's demand for family abolition, it is because it was first defeated, then actively erased. By 1981, Cheryl Clarke was sounding a little more isolated from mass movement, and perhaps a little unsure of herself (despite the bravado) when she wrote in the famous women-of-color anthology *This Bridge Called My Back*: "As far as I am concerned, any woman who calls herself a feminist must commit herself to the liberation of all women from coerced heterosexuality as it manifests itself in the family, the state, and on Madison Avenue."[54]

Ever since the capitalist victory over the long sixties, the shout for abolition of the family has been buried beneath a strange kind of shame: in Weeks's phrase, "feminists have tried to walk it back."[55] In a long cover feature for *Village Voice* in 1979, "The Family: Love It or Leave It," the revolutionary feminist Ellen Willis explicitly sets out to address this phenomenon: "the mentality that inspired veterans of the Sixties to say things like, 'We didn't succeed in abolishing the family. This proves we were wrong—the family is necessary.'"[56] The about-face was driving her nuts, she reported: at the close of the seventies, resigning themselves to their defeat, leftists were lapsing en masse into nostalgia, romanticizing the family and blaming capitalism for its collapse (when just ten years earlier they had been trashing the family and blaming capitalism for its persistence). Among her erstwhile comrades, she found there was suddenly an appetite not only for coupled bourgeois isolation but also for print justifications of it in the form of pro-family books such as *Haven in a Heartless World: The Family Besieged* (1977) by the erstwhile "neo-Marxist" and conservative moralist Christopher Lasch.

Willis's piece argued that the Left impulse to chest-beat and declare failure, albeit understandable, is indulgent. She reminded us, her people, that the experience of failure per se is a poor reason to decide the goals of the sixties were incorrect: "That we did not manage in a few years to revolutionize an institution that has lasted for thousands, serving indispensable functions as well as oppressive ones, is hardly something to be surprised at or ashamed of." We should not, in other words, be ashamed. Nor should we be surprised that the process of material and imaginative defeat that Willis was already documenting in the *Village Voice* before Thatcher came to power in Britain—and then Reagan in America—grew more entrenched in the years that followed. We would do well to remember: no matter how many neo-Laschian voices spring up around us—no matter how many fascoid ("red-brown") alliances and pseudo-Marxist-feminist "defenses of patriarchy"[57]—the thread can always be picked up, turned into a fuse, and lit.

Even deep in the desolation of the Eighties, Marxist feminists collaborated to keep the possibility of abolishing the family, alive, at least discursively. In 1983, Lynne Segal gathered and edited a collection entitled *What Is To be Done About the Family?* through the Socialist Society in Britain, which comprised sober reflections on contradictions in neoliberal childcare and the length of the road ahead from Mica Nava, Denise Riley and others.[58] In 1991, Barrett and McIntosh scandalized many on the British Left, firstly by speculating that "caring, sharing, and loving would be more widespread if the family did not claim them for its own,"[59] then by pointing out that the Labour Party's "familism" had lately actually exceeded that of Thatcher. McIntosh and Barrett's jointly authored book, *The Anti-Social Family*, mounted an enduringly powerful modern argument for the fundamental incompatibility of socialism and familism. "Privatized family collectivism tends to sap the strength of wider social collectivism," they explained painstakingly; "the stronger and more supportive families are expected to be, the weaker the other supportive institutions outside of them become."[60]

These feminists at this point were swimming against the current: most of their peers were pivoting and hastening to reassure distressed and outraged audiences that we aren't anti-family; in fact, we want more family, not less![61] This cowardly sleight of hand is understandable. I myself have participated in it on occasion, for instance, by agreeing that my first book, *Full Surrogacy Now: Feminism Against Family*, could be understood merely as a demand for more kinship. After all, when "family," at the very level of language, is synonymous with human connection, opposing it is taken to mean that you hate love.[62] Shulie, it has to be said, was not cowed by this charge. Even more so than Kollontai before her, she was prepared to say "down with love"[63]— actually existing love, that is—while yearning for the post-heterosexual, post-homosexual "healthy transsexuality" to come, which, she surmised, would transform the meaning of eroticism by diffusing it throughout society. Like Kollontai, this comrade had her sights set on a better, as-yet-unthinkable kind of love; red love. Firestone was a lover. By her friends' affectionate accounts, she loved sex with men very much. However, within present historic conditions, fighting for love necessarily means being a hater. Shulie helped sabotage bridal fairs, assailed beauty pageants, and earnestly floated the tactical possibility of a "smile boycott" (because *the smile [of] the child/woman ... indicates acquiescence of the victim to his own oppression*[64]). "Her detractors," notes Susan Faludi dryly, "accused her of homicidal tendencies."[65]

Besides editing and producing the short-lived, self-published militant (and millenarian) women's liberation journal *Notes*, our utopian killjoy forebear cofounded several revolutionary groups. New York Radical Women, Redstockings, and New York Radical Feminists sometimes carried out direct actions targeting, for instance, the offices of *Ladies' Home Journal*, copies of which Shulie ripped up in its editor's face. Fractious as these formations were, they changed uncountable women's lives forever. Heartbreakingly, immediately after the *Dialectic*'s release, however, Firestone deserted the world of politics for good. By some accounts, she came to believe feminism had "ruined her life."[66] Her big second book, intended to "lay the foundations of a powerful new women's art—with the potential to transform our very definition of culture"—never arrived. In 1998, a follow-up text appeared at last: *Airless Spaces*, a tiny, fragmentary collection of stories about the psychiatric incarceration of Shulamith and other inmates.[67] In 2012, Shulie died alone in her apartment. Thousands and thousands of her former comrades, gathered at memorials for her, recalled how impossible she was, in every sense.[68] Even those who couldn't really stand her bore passionate witness: Shulamith Firestone changed the world.

Gay and Lesbian—and Children's—Liberation

Few missed historic opportunities frustrate me more than the neglect of Shulie and her movement to link up—theoretically and practically—with Gay Liberation, the burgeoning parallel insurgency that championed the economic, sexual, and gender freedoms of young people, and attacked the private nuclear household "from the outside" (as Gay activists often put it). Opportunities for solidarity and conspiracy against the family had surely been presenting themselves from the early 1900s: the Euro-American family kept producing great numbers of fugitives in the form of girls and women fleeing rape, abuse, battery, or simply marriage, and homosexual, trans, or intersex youth kicked into the streets by their parents. Had the family abolitionism of Gay Lib collaborated, durably, with the family abolitionism of Women's Lib and Black Power, it seems to me, the lesbian-coined principle of "mothering against motherhood" (Adrienne Rich)[69] could have taken on new, gender- and whiteness-abolitionist potency. As it stands, we have largely disjointed genealogies of distinct oppressed communities' efforts to "learn to mother ourselves" (Audre Lorde's later phrase).[70] Writes queer historian Michael Bronski: "In the gay slang of the 1950s and '60s, an older gay man would be called 'mother' if he took on the task of guiding or advising newly-out young gay men."[71] The popularity of a positive (let alone utopian) theory of any-gendered *mothering* dwindled, however, as Gay organizing was forced, later in the century, into reacting to the catastrophic state of exception, community emergency, and hospice care-scarcity that was AIDS.[72]

Officially, Gay Liberation kicked off at Compton's Cafeteria, San Francisco, in August 1966, when drag queens and trans women associated with a group called Vanguard rioted against the policemen who systematically bashed and persecuted them.[73] The movement then went global in June 1969 with the anti-police riot at the Stonewall Inn, New York. In 1970, Stonewall veterans and Gay Liberation Front militants Sylvia Rivera, Marsha

P. Johnson, Bambi L'Amour, Bebe Scarpi, and others founded Street Transvestite Action Revolutionaries (STAR). Leaning on a Mafia acquaintance with real estate connections, they held a fundraiser and opened the transgender commune STAR House in the East Village, where the older transfeminine hustlers mothered dozens of newer refugees from the heteropatriarchal family at a time, building "Gay Power" and saving the lives of many transfeminine and/or queer youths they referred to as their "kids."[74] Meanwhile, back in San Francisco, the SDS organizer Carl Wittman was writing "Refugees from Amerika: A Gay Manifesto," in which he called on gays to aspire to more than "gay ghettos" and praised the emergence of "gay liberation communes," stating: "we must govern ourselves, set up our own institutions, defend ourselves, and use our won energies to improve our lives."[75] Concurrently, given their pathologization by experts (and even psychiatric torture and incarceration), gay and lesbian activists threw themselves into organizing "mad pride," patients' liberation and "anti-pyschiatry." A conference entitled "Schizo-Culture" united queers and neurodivergent "sickos" in challenging the power of parents and doctors.[76]

While precariously housed trans sex workers of color built technologies of survival in the cracks and margins of a homophobic and white-supremacist society, their immanent theories of gay liberation were going global. In 1971, the newly founded Front Homosexuel d'Action Révolutionnaire in France released a communiqué stating their intention to "explode the patriarchal family."[77] That same year, the GLF in London hammered out its manifesto. "Our entire society is built around the patriarchal family," they stated in their analysis:

The blueprint says "we two against the world," and that can be protective and comforting. But it can also be suffocating . . . Singly, or isolated in couples, we are weak—the way society wants us to be. Society cannot put us down so easily if we fuse together. We have to get together, understand one another, live together. . . . [But] our gay communes and collectives must not be mere convenient living arrangements or worse, just extensions of the gay ghetto. . . . We have to change our attitudes to our personal property, to our lovers, to our day-to day priorities in work and leisure, even to our need for privacy.[78]

As Gay Liberation gained momentum, these ideas began to concretize. In 1972, a group of activists drove down from Boston to the Democratic National Convention in Miami and leafleted attendees with their ten demands, many of which (abolition of the police, an end to US imperialism, among others) remain familiar today. Demand #6, however, is not something Democrats nowadays hear very often:

Rearing children should be the common responsibility of the whole community. Any legal rights parents have over "their" children should be dissolved and each child should be free to choose its own destiny. Free twenty-four hour child care centers should be established where faggots and lesbians can share the responsibility of child rearing.[79]

Many movements of the day, from Crip Liberation to Flower Power, were explicitly thinking about how to create solidarity with children. The Black Panthers established schools and intervened forcefully in the public school system by providing free breakfasts and after-school programs. Dozens of flavors of lesbian and feminist daycare centers—as well as unschooling ventures like Summerhill, as we saw—proliferated, some of them hopeful of starting a dialogue with children about what their liberation might mean.

By Bronski's count, at least fifteen US mass-market books promoted ideas of children's liberation and children's rights (including the right to have more than just one or two parents) throughout the seventies, including David Gottlieb's *Children's Liberation* (1973) and Beatrice and Ronald Gross's *The Children's Rights Movement: Overcoming the Oppression of Young People* (1977).[80] As Gumbs has shown, movement magazines like *Off Our Backs* included co-authored antiracist denunciations of "patriarchal ideas that say the children are owned by (property owning) parents." Interracial lesbian lovers Mary Peña and Barbara Carey, for example, declared: "[CHILDREN] WILL NOT BELONG TO THE PATRIARCHY / THEY WILL NOT BELONG TO US EITHER / THEY WILL BELONG ONLY TO THEMSELVES." In the same vein, at the National Third World Lesbian and Gay Conference of 1979—where Audre Lorde gave the keynote speech—a caucus of lesbians agreed on the statement: "All children of lesbians are ours."[81] In some cities, gay liberationists calling themselves Effeminists articulated the belief "that gay men should virtually place themselves in the service of women, taking on their traditional household tasks, including the raising of children, in order to foster women's rise to power." Some, following the example of the Women's Liberation movement's male militants, founded Men's Childcare Collectives.[82]

In the eighties, instead of standing up to the Reagan-era Moral Majority and Anita Bryant's homophobic "Save Our Children" crusade, which equated gay life with pedophilia, the bulk of the movement backed away from any connection with children and concentrated instead on surviving AIDS. The aim of exploding the nuclear family was replaced by a rights-only agenda that eventually gave renewed life to the nuclear family by reinvesting in its symbolic and practical necessity. Then, in the wake of the avoidable mass HIV-induced death wreaked among queers by Reagan's Plague, a new "homonormative" gay subject emerged on the American scene—erotically continent, creditable, productive, potentially parental. Today (exactly as with feminism) other than among the fringes of religious evangelism, the proposition that LGBTQ interests might threaten marriage or have anything to do with challenging the family is unknown. In some metropoles, the type of bourgeois homosexuality ("straight gayness") identified as an enemy by Gay Libbers early on is now quasi-hegemonic. The gay family—which Gay Power hoped to render an oxymoron—has become a decisive factor in the family's salvation.

Wages for Housework and the National Welfare Rights Organization

A little after the time when Gay Liberation was kicking off in the United States, a group of "autonomist" Marxist feminists in Italy launched the Wages for Housework Campaign. The original group was spearheaded by Leopoldina Fortunati and Mariarosa Dalla Costa; soon enough, their comrades in Canada, England, and New York—including Selma James, Silvia Federici, Margaret Prescod and Nicole Cox—helped coordinate the proliferation of branches of the network, culminating in the International Wages for Housework Committee. Subgroups such as Wages Due Lesbians, the English Collective of Prostitutes, and Black Women for Wages for Housework soon formed. What was the task at hand? Organizing a planetary women's strike, a seizure of the means of reproduction (seizure of cold hard cash, at least to begin with). It didn't matter if society agreed that wages were, in fact, owed for women's labor. As the slogan enjoined: *Women of all ages, collect your wages!* Wages for Housework was "serving notice" to "all governments." They demanded the entirety of the money due to their sex "in full and retroactive." Wages for Housework came up with a remarkably precise dictum to convey their perspective on the activities performed by so many women in their own homes: "They say it is love. We say it is unwaged work."[83] Pointedly, they *did not deny* that unwaged childcare, eldercare, housekeeping, sex, emotional labor, wifehood, might be a manifestation of love. Rather, the militants argued that "nothing so effectively stifles our lives as the transformation into work of the activities and relations that satisfy our desires."[84] Put differently: the fact that caring for a private home under capitalism often *is* an expression of loving desire, while at the same time being life-choking work, is precisely the problem. That the "they" of the dictum—bosses, husbands, dads—are not wrong about this illustrates the insidiousness of the violence careworkers encounter (and mete out) in the family-form. It's the reason paid and unpaid domestics, and paid and unpaid mothers, still have to fight just to be seen as workers. And why being recognized as workers remains only a precursor to—one day—ending their exploitation and, by extension, beginning to know a new and different form of love, just as Kollontai envisioned it: a love *beyond the family*.

Under capitalism, Wages for Housework perceived, "love" often serves the interests of the ruling class because it can be leveraged to depress wages (*surely you're not in this for the money*) or even withhold them altogether (*do what you love and you'll never work a day in your life*). The gendered injunction to care "for love, not money" obscures the grinding, repetitive, invisible, energy-sapping, confining aspects of the work involved in making homes of any kind. The principle that some things "should not be for sale" becomes a way to disguise the reality that, everywhere, on every street, they are—and to excuse underpaying those doing the "selling." Thus the Wages for Housework movement was not *for* housework at all. On the contrary: these workers were against it, against wages, and against all capitalist work for that matter. Their platform—which was rephrased and clarified by Federici in the formula "wages *against* housework"[85]—was in this sense far removed from the now-ascendant demand that we "value" care work and grant "dignity" to domestic labor. In my reading, it was family-abolitionist.

In parallel, and with the frequent collaboration of Wages for Housework, in the United States, welfare recipients organized in hundreds of local groups across the country, eventually coalescing under the umbrella of the National Welfare Rights Organization (NWRO), which at its peak represented as many as one hundred thousand people.[86] Between 1966 and 1975, the massed efforts of the NWRO—the majority of whom were African American women—reshaped the food stamps program, made the welfare application process more accountable, expanded programs available to poor women and children, and generally fought the ruling class in the name, not of work or of family, but of proletarian female deserving. "While it was certainly necessary for poor Black women to represent and classify themselves as families that were eligible for public assistance from the AFDC program to survive," writes King in "Abolishing Moynihan's Negro Family," they simultaneously *contested* "the objectification of Black households and Black people through the social scientific discourse of the family."[87]

One of the West Coast women behind the founding of NWRO was Johnnie Tillmon, a self-defined *middle-aged, poor, fat, Black woman on welfare*. In an article for *Ms.* magazine in 1972, Tillmon wrote: "For a lot of middle-class women in this country, Women's Liberation is a matter of concern. For women on welfare, it's a matter of survival." Welfare, she explained:

is the most prejudiced institution in this country, even more than marriage, which it tries to imitate. ... A.F.D.C. (Aid to Families with Dependent Children) says if there is an "able-bodied" man around, then you can't be on welfare. If the kids are going to eat, and the man can't get a job, then he's got to go.

Welfare is like a super-sexist marriage. You trade in a man for *the* man. But you can't divorce him if he treats you bad. He can divorce you, of course, cut you off anytime he wants. But in that case, *he* keeps the kids, not you. *The* man runs everything.

In ordinary marriage, sex is supposed to be for your husband. On AFDC, you're not supposed to have any sex at all. You give up control of your own body. It's a condition of aid. You may even have to agree to get your tubes tied so you can never have more children just to avoid being cut off welfare.[88]

Not only did Tillmon refuse to countenance the family as a true escape from the persecution of the state; she also rejected the idea that waged work could liberate women of her class. At a time when many feminists were concentrating their efforts on gaining access to the workplace, Tillmon and her comrades, just like Wages for Housework, demanded, simply, dollars: the freedom to *not* work. Sick and tired of exploitative jobs, poverty wages, and intrusive, paternalistic, stingy public programs, welfare activists took to the streets, picketed the welfare centers, and packed the courts, propelled by "the aspiration that women's lives would no longer be dictated by husbands, employers, government bureaucrats, and clerks," in the words of Wilson Sherwin and Frances Fox Piven.[89] Not content to defend the right to stay home, they challenged the notion that staying at home or working are the only options available to women.

In 1968, NWRO's vice-president, Beulah Sanders, a hell-raising New Yorker, had co-organized the Poor People's Campaign (which camped out on Washington Mall for six weeks) with Martin Luther King. In May 1970, Sanders and Tillmon together led a sit-in protest at the office for Health, Education and Welfare (HEW).

According to the *New York Times* coverage of the takeover, Sanders sat in the relevant US Secretary Robert H. Finch's "leather chair for seven hours of 'liberation' with the title of 'Acting H.E.W. Secretary.'"[90] Beulah called, from this chair, for an end to the US military occupation of Southeast Asia, and a universal basic income of at least $5,500 per annum ("Give poor people enough money to live decently, and let us decide how to live our lives").[91] Equally, she began honing her critique of *commodified and uncommodified* housework, asking in 1972: "Is it fair to call a woman lazy who stays at home, cooks, washes, irons, cleans house, teaches her kids how to do things, and helps them with their homework? If she does the same work for somebody else for $2.00 or less an hour is she really a better woman? You tell me."[92] For this analysis, I have been especially inspired by King's and Sherwin and Piven's argument: that, while some in the NWRO did demand money on the basis of redemptive, *maternalist* arguments, many did not. I submit we view the NWRO, and Wages for Housework, as family-abolitionist organizations on the basis of their simultaneously (or combined) non-maternal and non-workerist accounts of what it is that a poor single mom needs and wants.

Twenty-First-Century Trans Marxism

There was a thirty-year lull in family-abolitionism between 1985 and 2015. While family abolition is still scoffed at by many people—including on the anticapitalist left—today, there are once more sincere conversations blossoming in diverse forums ranging from socialist ones like *Tribune* magazine's podcast "Politics Theory

Other"[93] and *Jacobin* magazine's "The Dig"[94] to art galleries and mainstream media vehicles like Vice Media and the *New Yorker*. Speaking as a free-lance writer, I can attest that COVID-19's exacerbation of the care crisis played a big role in the openness of editors—if not the general public—to hear criticisms of the private nuclear household. (Even the *Times* columnist David Brooks was inspired to write 9,000 words under the heading "The Nuclear Family Was a Mistake" in *The Atlantic* in 2020—albeit Brooks only wanted to reform the historic "mistake" of the family ever so slightly.[95]) I am self-evidently not impartial, having published an attempted Marxian transfeminist family-abolition manifesto once before. Yet it seems clear to me that we, the exponents of "transgender Marxism" and "abolition feminism," are driving the resurgence.[96]

The current "wave"—if I can optimistically call it that—began, as far as I am aware, in 2015 with the aforementioned co-authored manifesto "Kinderkommunismus: A Feminist Analysis of the 21st-Century Family and a Communist Proposal for Its Abolition." The proposal, if you recall, is for a "revolutionary crèche": an institution of social reproduction that would feed all, abolish deprivation, and undo the people's capitalism-induced mindset of desperation and scarcity (Jules and Kate note ruefully that this "presupposes a communist revolution").[97] In 2018, the queer and gender studies scholar Tiffany Lethabo King's article on "Abolishing Moynihan's Negro Family" came out, as it were, for family abolitionism, arguing that practices of Black world-making "must envision life outside of the current categories that blunt efforts to re-craft what it means to be human."[98] M. E. O'Brien's ongoing work on the subject appeared in Commune magazine ("Six Steps to Abolish the Family"), Pinko ("Communizing Care"), and Endnotes ("The Working Class Family and Gender Liberation in Capitalist Development") throughout 2019, 2020, and 2021, as did mine[99] and that of Gleeson,[100] Katie Stone,[101] Alva Gotby,[102] Sophie Silverstein,[103] Zoe Belinsky,[104] Alyson Escalante,[105] and others. Much to my excitement, the celebrated philosopher of (anti-) work, Kathi Weeks, participated in an "Abolish the Family!" panel at the Seattle-based yearly festival Red May in 2020,[106] before releasing her scholarly paper on the contemporary relevance of family-abolitionism in Feminist Theory the following year.[107] Every other week, a study group, mutual aid cluster, DIY radio program, theater ensemble, art collective, or free university in Italy, Denmark, Norway, Slovenia, Greece, The Netherlands, Britain, Ireland, Portugal, Switzerland, Brazil, France, Germany, Japan, Korea, Russia, and Spain, gets in touch to inform me about their "family abolition" programming. An online course I offered on Family Abolition, via the Brooklyn Institute for Social Research, was oversubscribed in 2021 and again in April of 2022.[108] The magnificent anthology Las degeneradas trans acaban contra la familia, or Trans Degenerates Abolish the Family, edited by Ira Hybris, has just appeared in Spain. Momentum is undeniably growing. The art world is seizing on these ideas (a development I welcome, albeit with a little apprehension, because the art world can be where insurgencies go to die).

Some of the most recent statements of twenty-first-century yearning take us, beautifully, right back to the beginning of this story. "Charles Fourier," for O'Brien, "was a delightfully kinky science fiction writer, and an inspiration to imagining pro-queer communes of the future." In her pamphlet-length piece on Fourier, she compares his phalanstery size of 1,600 people with that of a 2016 proposal from the London-based group Angry Workers of the World for "domestic units comprising 200 to 250 people." The Angry Workers estimate of around 200 people "strikes me as reasonable, perhaps preferable," O'Brien writes: "Two hundred could be a sizable apartment building, the stand-alone homes clustered immediately around a school or other center, or a block of small apartment buildings. The shared kitchen would create a natural initial size, given the logistics of cooking for substantial groups."

Amid present conditions of suffocating anti-utopianism, it strikes me as a matter of some considerable urgency to practice educating our desire by speculating concretely about the architectures, challenges, timelines, infrastructures and affects of family abolition—an endeavor O'Brien and Eman Abdelhadi pursue even more seriously in their co-authored 2022 novel *Everything For Everyone: An Oral History of the New York Commune, 2052–2072*.[109] Rather than coming about as the implementation of an anal plan for absolute harmony, O'Brien knows, the inevitably chaotic commune "could arise spontaneously out of insurrection."[110]

4
Comrades Against Kinship

"Any critique of the family is usually greeted with, 'but what would you put in its place?' We hope that by now it will be clear that we would put nothing in the place of the family."

— Michèle Barrett and Mary McIntosh[1]

When economic crises and/or pandemics strike, it is paradoxically our scarcities that we want to hug to ourselves, lest they be taken away. So engrained is the logic of the private household, for example, we almost did not need to be told, back in February 2020, that a person's first line of defense against the coronavirus is her private property with its roster of registered relatives. The state's presupposition in tackling the COVID-19 pandemic has been brutally clear: there is no alternative to the family. Populations were mandated to keep a "social distance" (from everyone . . . except family) and to "shelter in place" (in whose place? our family's, of course). Many adults "boomeranged," as the papers called it: moving back into their parents' homes during the pandemic.[2] But how could a zone defined by the asymmetries of power—of reproductive labor, marriage (often), and patriarchal parenting, by rent and mortgage debt—benefit health? Abusers everywhere predictably battered and molested their partners and "dependents" with increased impunity, in the privacy of their apartments, since it was more difficult than ever, physically and financially, to exit a home.

Nevertheless, the dearth of alternatives meant that COVID-19 also exacerbated the exclusion and marginalization of the disowned, the propertyless, the unhoused, the warehoused, the web-illiterate and those without pre-existing privacy—in short, those of us we are encouraged to think of as (unlike oneself, or at least *more so*) homeless. It's no joke, having no "place," no municipally legible place to shelter in, under a policy of shelter-in-place. In my town, it was the vagrant, Black, sex-working, substance-using people, the young street queers, and the unpropertied generally who were systematically brutalized by police for defying COVID-19 directives. Nevertheless, it was far from clear, in my town—particularly in light of high reported contamination rates in the prisons and so-called homeless shelters—that sleeping under bricks and mortar with one's legal relatives was epidemiologically (or otherwise) prudent. Indeed, the whole framing of the indoors, sticking with one's "folks," and so on, as the key to the lockdown, appeared upon closer inspection deeply equivocal. It depended on a public/private double standard that went, for the most part, unexplained.

Stay within your clan and dwelling, ran the edict; but whereas, when it comes to the public realm, the vaporous mass of your always-partially-aerosolized body must strive to remain outdoors, in the private realm, conversely, it must be kept indoors as much as possible. A household breathes and dies together in its owned or rented property. If you live at no fixed address, in the cracks between commodified buildings, under bridges, or in parks, you are defying virus-management directives, even if your exposure risk is vanishingly small. The virus is a stranger danger. Your pod is your safety. Do not, do *not*, riot all summer long in the open air.

I learned something disorienting from the months-long 2020 tent encampment on the scenic Franklin Parkway, a boulevard in central Philly, variously dubbed Camp Maroon, Camp Teddy and Camp JTD.[3] What was Camp Maroon? An occupation, complete with a kitchen, distribution center, medical tent, substance use supply store, and even a jerry-rigged standing shower—a militant village led by unhoused Philadelphians and working-class rebels like the indomitable, one-in-a-million Jennifer Bennetch (rest in power).[4] The encampment was composed of hundreds of people willing to live together side by side, in tents, to struggle for free housing, migrant freedoms, the right to the city, and more. Even I, standing on the periphery, felt transformed. It was that summer that taught me this: *all beings exploited by capital and by empire are basically homeless.*[5] All of us have been driven from the commons. Everywhere, humans have woven enclaves and cradles of possibility, relief, and reciprocity in the desert. But the thing that would make our houses *home*—in a new, true, common sense of the word—is a practice of planetary revolution.

It might seem a bit vertiginous to draw such huge conclusions from a localized camp-out in the middle of Pennsylvania's capital city.[6] But if you have experienced, even just for a few days, the alternate social world that brews in the utopian squatting of a city boulevard, you probably know. It's trippy: people acquire a tiny taste of collective self-governance, of mutual protection and care, and suddenly, the list of demands, objectives, targets and desires becomes much longer and more ambitious than simply "affordable housing." That's why M. E. O'Brien thinks "the best starting point to abolish the family" is the protest kitchen: "Form self-organized, shared sleeping areas for safety. Set up cooperative childcare to support the full involvement of parents. Establish syringe exchanges and other harm reduction practices to welcome active drug users."[7] Expand from there, and never stop expanding.

Toward the end of 2020, the City of Philadelphia made some substantial housing-related concessions, then forcibly cleared Camp Maroon. As its memory—as well as that of the city-wide George Floyd insurrections—started to fade, the media hurried to emphasize the supposedly universal reality of attrition into fully-remote, podded, stay-the-fuck-at-home life. Pandemic insurance benefits gave a material reprieve to hundreds of thousands. Confirmed infections citywide approached 150,000. Health workers and other sacrificial "front liners," as well as home-based care-givers, began burning out. As 2021 dragged on, fully housed yet underserved students and workers—especially of color—turned increasingly to suicide. In the age of lockdowns, many met a fate worse than forced time with family, namely: not having a family.

I am writing this, in early 2022, almost a year into a period of job-quitting and work-stoppage widely known as "The Great Resignation" or even "The Great Refusal." In many parts of the US, proponents of forced gestation have succeeded in destroying the right to stop performing gestational labor. Christian-nationalism is on a rampage, proposing that trans children, for instance, shall be kinless (legislators in Texas this year equated trans-affirming childcare with child abuse and proposed it be grounds for child removal).[8] The family is being re-disciplined. What will happen next?

So far, this little book has introduced the emotional panic and political promise of family abolitionism, argued against setting aside a particular kind of family to be saved from abolition, and surveyed its history to date. My hope is that you now agree that moving beyond the family—as opposed to "expanding" it—is desirable. It is time to grasp the nettle, then, and consider what *abolition* means in practice. The answer is surprisingly complicated, even though the word is lately being broadcast around the world and spelled out in giant letters once more on the tarmac outside police precincts via the movement of hundreds of thousands of feet.

From where I am standing—a viewpoint which, admittedly, is likely to be Anglocentric—it seems as though the specific term "abolition" has been taken back up in a big way. We have entered a moment of abolition fervor and generalized abolitionism on a scale that was last seen in the nineteenth century. This upswell represents a magnificent outcome of at least ten years of grassroots agitation in the belly of the beast of American empire, in tandem with other struggles: Palestine's, for example. "Abolish prisons," "abolish ICE," and "abolish the police" became familiar demands and credible concepts attached to popular platforms. To be sure, some pundits cannot believe their ears. You can't possibly mean *abolish*!? Because, on its face, the answer to this question is almost comically self-evident: what do abolitionists want? Abolitionists want to abolish. We want things not to be. We want an absence of prisons, of colonizers. We desire the nonexistence of police.

Simple, right? Not according to the earliest originators and modern philosopher-activists of abolition (and we should now briefly register the word *abolition*'s weighty original German form, *Aufhebung*). In English translations of the early nineteenth-century writings of German idealist G. W. F. Hegel, *Aufhebung* is sometimes translated as "positive supersession," and intriguingly, this rather stiff bit of jargon unites the ideas of lifting up, destroying, preserving, and radically transforming, all at once. These four components can be illustrated with reference to slavery, the earliest example of a radical cause calling itself "abolitionist" in history. The successful global fight for the abolition of slavery meant that the noble ideal of humanism, trumpeted in the French Revolution, was simultaneously lifted up (vindicated), destroyed (exposed as white), preserved (made tenable for the future) and transformed beyond recognition (forced to incorporate those it had originally excluded). Slavery was overturned in law and eventually more or less done away with in practice. What we must understand, however, is that our very capacity to understand these events was generated *by them*. In the "before" times, the ideals that governed slave-trading societies really *were* human rights, life, liberty, and the pursuit of happiness. The world manifested those ideas as they existed then, until, at the end of an enslaved person's rifle, the self-styled inventors of "freedom" in these societies learned at last what real freedom (a *more real* freedom, for the time being) looked like. Humanism: negated, remade, born, buried, prolonged. By winning the struggle against slavers, abolition gave the lie to those societies, and supplied those brave ideals with their first-ever shot at becoming more than words.

That is *Aufhebung*, as I understand it, and it's an understanding I owe to the expansive teachings of, among others, above all, Ruth Wilson Gilmore. The abolition of prisons and of the police, rather than constituting a simple deletion of infrastructure, is better understood as a world-building endeavor, a collective act of creativity without end, giving rise to real justice where, before, there had been Justice with a capital 'J'. At its most basic level, says Gilmore, abolition "is not the absence of something; it's the presence of something. That's what abolition actually is."[9] To practice abolition, we are required to "change one thing: everything."[10] While Gilmore does not focus on kinship questions, there is no question in my mind that the horizon of abolition entails changing everything about the family, too. *What would it mean to not need the family?*

So, what can we say, now, about the destruction-preser-vation-transformation-realization of the family, in light of these brief thoughts on how struggle unfolds? We might remark, first of all, that a process of "changing everything" *could not* leave the family intact even if it wanted to. Secondly, we could seek to isolate that which is liberatory about the kinship-ideal, buried within the material misery that is familialized society. What is it that is presently travestied, yet worth realizing? In the case of familiality, the latent utopian kernels seem to be:

reciprocal care, interdependence, and belonging. These are the mass desires buried inside a casket labeled "exclusivity," "chauvinism," "race," "property," "heredity," "identity," "competition." Anyone can glimpse them, these ideal versions of family values smothered in everyday life. They're iterated emptily in everything from fashion branding to ecological ethics symposia. All around us, we can glimpse the filaments of the family's dialectical explosion: *Maria our cleaner is part of the family,*[11] *here at Olive Garden <u>everyone</u> is family, we're all family here at TrustAir™ (because we care), say hello to the great family of humanity, we use 30% renewable energy because the island's endangered birds are family, the great planetary family, family is as family does, welcome to the city of brotherly love, we believe in kinship between all living things.*

Bullshit. Imagine what would have to happen in order for the staff at restaurants and airlines to be welcome to input your name as a guarantor for their student debt. Consider what would make the fashion retailer Kinship™ (whose website currently celebrates "the bond we share," and states that "we are all kin") turn up to an eviction defense on your behalf. Ask yourself what needs to change before Maria the cleaner is able to add her name to the children's birth certificates if she wants to. Then ask yourself whether birth certificates are really necessary. If these thought experiments seem silly, we have to consider the possibility that kinship, as a value, isn't worth all that much. Let me be more direct: I don't particularly like what kinship affords us, ethically or politically. I don't think it is doing a lot of good. What is worse, I think it is getting in the way of better possibilities.

Don't get me wrong: I appreciate that our quasi-universal desire for kinship mediates a desire for care, no more no less. It is not our collective desire for care that I am criticizing; it is the insufficiency of the vehicle we have at our disposal for that desire's realization. Without wading into the weeds of anthropological debates around definition of kinship—or, for that matter, anthropological debates about *whether* it is important to define kinship—I submit that kinship, at least right now, is always a reference to something that is imagined to be inerasable; to "nature." Perhaps one day it will be fit for purpose again, who knows? Perhaps because the concept of nature has itself been turned inside out. But right now, even when it is conceptualized as practice-based (as it is in many Indigenous cosmologies), kinship functions as a linguistic appeal to something *non-contingent* that can ground a relation. And I am asking: can we suspend that fantasy of something non-contingent? Can we let go of it?

Before the twenty-first century, Donna Haraway—the philosopher to whom I owe my feminism—was not advocating "kinmaking." Quite the contrary, in fact. "I am sick to death," she said in 1997, "of bonding through kinship and 'the family'":

and I long for models of solidarity and human unity and difference rooted in friendship, work, partially shared purposes, intractable collective pain, inescapable mortality, and persistent hope. It is time to theorize an 'unfamiliar' unconscious, a different primal scene, where everything does not stem from the dramas of identity and reproduction. Ties through blood—including blood recast in the coin of genes and information—have been bloody enough already. I believe that there will be no racial or sexual peace, no livable nature, until we learn to produce humanity through something more and less than kinship.[12]

Just as I am changing my tune here with regard to the line "real families against the family" (a distillation I started offering audiences of the thesis of Full Surrogacy Now, which Haraway generously read), Haraway's recent work on "making kin" is a departure from her own conclusions—above—about the material semiotics of kinship. Not for the first time, I am plumping for the earlier Haraway.[13]

The kinship-value, despite its potentially radical aspiration to encompass the whole world and all the beings in it, is functionally unusable, I think. It is, in the current moment, just a cute frontispiece over the family. When you drill down into it, *blood being thicker than water* is always and perhaps inevitably kin-talk's central referent and underlying metaphor. Thus, I submit, taking family abolitionism seriously requires a serious and concerted effort to loosen, unseat, and unlearn the thought, practice, and language of "kinship." It is a simple argument, and one others before me have expressed more pithily: "It is the belief that kinship, love and having nice things to eat are naturally and inevitably bound up together that makes it hard to imagine a world in which 'family' plays little part."[14] These, as you may know already, are the words of Michèle Barrett and Mary McIntosh, whose tremendous answer to the question "What would you put in the place of the family?" was, simply: "Nothing."

If we hold hands, we can certainly be brave enough to step into the abundance that will be the nothingness that comes after the family.

No thanks, right? Don't we all have enough contingency going on, as it is, in the maw of the care crisis that is capitalism? Surely the last thing we want to do is ask our loved ones to embrace even *more* contingency! I have no doubt about it: so acute is our care scarcity, the only way we really know how to offer security to one another right now is by pretending that our love is non-contingent. When I say to you that you are "family," or that I think of you as "kin," I am saying "I love you, I care for you, I insure you, I hold you, I see you"—yes—and/but I am underlining this by using a metaphor that means I have no real choice about the matter. I am giving you a *guarantee* (*we are kin*) tethered to a metaphysical plane. And this feels good! At least, it is supposed to feel good. But obviously, an uncomradely hierarchy is baked right into this entire thought structure. *Real* kin will always be realer.

We can talk about extending kinship to the whole world all we want. If kinship were truly something we valued as *made*, not given, we wouldn't have to specify the word "chosen" (as in: "chosen kinship" or "chosen family") when we are talking about kinship that *isn't* imaginable as governmentally ratified (marriage or guardianship based), genetic, or bloodborne.

We need concepts with more bite, concepts like "comradeliness" or "accomplice." Or, if we want something intermediary, we could also consider resurrecting the defunct first half of the still-familiar Old English phrase "kith and kin." The concept of "kith" denotes a form of dynamic relation between beings, a bond similar to "kin," but one whose ground is knowledge, practice, and place, rather than race, descent, and identity. (In her essay "Make Kith, Not Kin!" McKenzie Wark speaks of *kith*'s "nebulous senses of the friend, neighbor, local, and the customary."[15]) What if we reacquainted ourselves with it, and attempted to gently edge out the primacy of kinship, with which *kith* obviously massively overlaps? The family won't be unmade in language, but nor is the semiotic separable from the material (and I am not prepared to hammer out policy interventions in this chapter). We might be surprised by how much humanity becomes possible when we cease "treating one another like family." At the same time, Patricia Hill Collins is right to point out that the language and thought structure of kinship— "brother," "sister," "mama," "Father," "child"—occupies such a prominent place in liberation traditions, that "rejecting it outright might be counterproductive for groups aiming to challenge hierarchies."[16] There are no comfortable strategies here. As Ellen Willis suggests, "to refuse to fight for love that is both free and responsible is in a sense to reject the possibility of love itself."[17]

We do not have to reject the language of kinship outright. Collectively, rather, we can begin to torque it. It's time to practice being kith or, better, comrades— including toward members of our "biofam"—building structures of dependency, need, and provision with no kinship dimension.

Caring, sharing, and loving are at present to be sought, depended upon, and expected pretty much *only* in kinship contexts. This amounts to a tragic, intricate orchestration of artificial insufficiency, and it has made our appetite for utopia dwindle down to almost nothing. "It is very, very difficult," wrote Linda Gordon, "to conceive of a society in which children do not belong to someone or ones. To make children the property of the state would be no improvement. Mass, state-run day care centers are not the answer." Do we have answers? Do we know yet which kinds of relation are outside capitalist accumulation? Lou Cornum: "If the answer today is none, let us devise some by tomorrow."[18] Let us devise some by tomorrow while, at the same time, as Kathi Weeks says, meditating on "what it means to commit to the long game of radical structural transformation that family abolitionism requires; even if we might be among the agents that help to bring that different future into being, we will not be, and perhaps could not be, the subjects fully desirous of that world."[19] The people we currently call children, whose "fertile" or "deviant" bodies are presently once more the standard and battleground for a violently queerphobic familism, must be among those at the very center of this long-haul metamorphosis.

"The nuclear family turns children into property," writes Lola Olufemi in her paean to diasporic Black revolutionary feminism *Experiments in Imagining Otherwise*.[20] As a matter of urgency, let us take this to heart, opening anew what Lola calls "the possibility that we could reorganize the family and the buildings we live in and the food we eat and the education we receive and start taking things for free in order to raise children in ways that make sacrifice or regret or biological drives or gendered alienation impossible."[21] I don't have to tell you this, but: it is good to protest and riot against "family separations" especially when young people and their companions are being ripped apart and warehoused in cages in their thousands rather than helped to make the crossing over arbitrary lines on the earth. Forced family reunification is not always a good thing, and can even be lethal to some people, but the separational techniques of the border of any nation-state are the very heart of the family regime. Border-torture tramples and even *targets* kin-relationships in part to uphold the fiction that the nation-state respects the integrity of families once they have been admitted. Border guards do not somehow abolish the family, they are its prime enforcers. Fighting the family regime might thus look like several different things: prising the state's boot off the neck of a "legal" family of "aliens," for instance, and at the same time offering solidarity to a queer kid in that same family, should she need it, against her parents.

What we are saying is that we have to do both at once: make the state return especially dependent humans to the arms of the few caregivers it tends to recognize *and* insist on deprivatizing care, contesting "parental rights," and imagining a world in which all people are cared for by many by default. What we are saying is that KEEPING FAMILIES TOGETHER and ENDING FAMILY SEPARATION are political imperatives and calls to action for all white race traitors, yet, still, they are not our horizon. *Being together as people* and ending the separation of *people*—this is a future that can be imagined, even if it cannot be fully desired yet, at least, not by us. I don't know how to desire it fully, but I can't wait to see what comes after the family. I also know I probably won't see whatever it is. Still, I hope it happens, and I hope it is a glorious and abundant nothing.

Notes

1 But I Love My Family!

1 King, Tiffany Lethabo, 2018. "Black 'Feminisms' and Pessimism: Abolishing Moynihan's Negro Family," *Theory & Event* 21(1): 68–87.

2 Shulamith Firestone herself—the woman who at times knew better than anybody that *everything* was possible, and that the family, along with the sex-distinction itself, had to be eradicated–wrote a letter to her sister Laya in 1970 in which she expressed her unwillingness to unmake her selfhood: "*I don't believe finally that the revolution is so imminent that it's worth tampering with my whole psychological structure.*" Quoted in Susan Faludi, "Death of a Revolutionary," *The New Yorker*, April 8, 2013, newyorker.com.

3 Anne McClintock, *Imperial Leather*, New York: Routledge, 1995, 45. See also Patricia Hill Collins, "It's All in the Family: Intersections of Gender, Race and Nation," *Hypatia* 13(3): 62–82, 1998. Collins extends McClintock's point to the US context: "Families are expected to socialize their members into an appropriate set of 'family values' that simultaneously reinforce the hierarchy within the assumed unity of interests symbolized by the family and lay the foundation for many social hierarchies" (64).

4 Mario Mieli, *Towards a Gay Communism*, transl. Evan Calder Williams. London: Pluto, 2018, 5.

5 Melinda Cooper, *Family Values: Between Neoliberalism and the New Social Conservatism*, New York: Zone Books, 2017, 1.

6 On this point, Andreas Chatzidakis, Jamie Hakim, Jo Littler, Catherine Rottenberg, and Lynne Segal note that "the neoliberal insistence on only taking care of yourself and your closest kin also leads to a paranoid form of 'care for one's own' that has become one of the launch pads for the recent rise of hard-right populism across the globe." The Care Collective, *The Care Manifesto: The Politics of Interdependence,* London: Verso, 2020.

7 Seymour points out that, even if Arthur had been able to speak to a social worker by himself, the institutions that might have helped "tend to defer to parents. Their bias is toward keeping families together. . . . The default is that children should depend for almost all their material resources, love and care, on whatever can be provided by at most two parents based on their own family experiences, education and remuneration from the labour market. Those are the rules. That's how class is transmitted. And it's a far from optimal situation for child safety." Richard Seymour, "Naming Your Laws After Dead Children," Patreon, December 10, 2021, patreon.com.

8 Of family abolitionism, Seymour writes, in the wake of a social media uproar sparked by publicity for this book: "it is an idea with a long tradition on the socialist Left that deserves to be debated. It is not a petty-bourgeois affectation of the activist Left. It is not a silly woke extravagance. It is not posturing pseudo-radicalism." Richard Seymour, "Notes on a Normie Shitstorm," *Salvage,* January 27, 2022, salvage.zone.

9 Ursula K. Le Guin, 2004, "All Happy Families," 33–45 in *The Wave in the Mind: Talks and Essays on the Writer, the Reader, and the Imagination,* Boulder, CO: Shambhala.

10 Michèle Barrett and Mary McIntosh, *The Anti-Social Family*, London: Verso Books, 1991, 48.

11 Emily Oster, *The Family Firm: A Data-Driven Guide to Better Decision Making in the Early School Years*, New York: Penguin, 2021, 90.

12 M. E. O'Brien covers the workers' movement's demand for a family wage in depth in her *Endnotes* essay "To Abolish the

Family," 2020. She summarizes: "This family form [i.e. male-breadwinner or 'housewife-based'] was a tremendous victory in improving the standard of living and survival of millions of working-class people, and creating a basis for stable neighbourhood organization, sustained socialist struggle and major political victories. It was also the means by which the workers' movement would distinguish itself from the lumpenproletariat, black workers, and queers."

13 For indispensable analysis of the imperiled "sacred child" in catastrophe and Anthropocene discourses, see: Rebekah Sheldon, *The Child to Come: Life After the Human Catastrophe*, Minneapolis: University of Minnesota Press, 2016. On how pediatric care cissexualized and racialized juvenile bodies, see: Jules Gill-Peterson, *Histories of the Transgender Child*, Minneapolis: University of Minnesota Press, 2018.

14 Sally Rooney (2021) *Beautiful World, Where Are You*, New York: Farrar, Straus and Giroux. For an astute review, see: Sarah Brouillette, "The Consolations of Heterosexual Monogamy in Sally Rooney's *Beautiful World, Where Are You*," *Blind Field*, September 30, 2021.

15 For the definitive analysis of horror cinema's theorization of domestic work under capitalism via the "care strike," see: Johanna Isaacson, *Stepford Daughters: Tools for Feminists in Contemporary Horror*, Philadelphia: Common Notions, 2022. Other texts include Isaacson's essay "Riot Horror" in *Theory & Event*, 2019; Dana Heller's *Family Plots*, University of Pennsylvania, 1995; Barry K. Grant's edited collection *The Dread of Difference: Gender and the Horror Film*, University of Texas, 1996; and Miranda Brady's article "'I think the men are behind it': reproductive labour and the horror of second wave feminism," *Feminist Media Studies*, 2021.

16 Tony Williams, *Hearths of Darkness*, University Press of Mississippi, 1996.

17 O'Brien, M. E., "6 Steps to Abolish the Family," *Commune*, December 30, 2019. communemag.com.

18 Hardt, Michael, 2017. "Red Love," *South Atlantic Quarterly*, 116 (4), 781.

2 Abolish Which Family?

1 Hortense Spillers, "Mama's Baby, Papa's Maybe: An American Grammar Book," *diacritics* 17(2): 64–81, 1987, 80.

2 Tiffany Lethabo King, "Abolishing Moynihan's Negro Family," 2018, 69.

3 King, 2018, 69.

4 Alexis Pauline Gumbs, China Martens, and Mai'a Williams (eds.) *Revolutionary Mothering: Love on the Front Lines*, Oakland: PM Press, 2016; Carol Stack, *All Our Kin: Strategies for Survival in a Black Community*, New York: Harper and Row, 1974.

5 Jennifer Nash, "The Political Life of Black Motherhood," *Feminist Studies* 44(3): 699–712, 2018, 11. See also Nash's book-length expansion on this theme: *Birthing Black Mothers*, Durham: Duke University Press, 2021.

6 Alexis Pauline Gumbs, "'We Can Learn to Mother Ourselves': The Queer Survival of Black Feminism," PhD dissertation, Duke University, 2010, 63.

7 Hazel Carby, "White Woman Listen! Black Feminism and the Boundaries of Sisterhood," 45–53 in Heidi Mirza (ed.) *Black British Feminism: A Reader*, London: Routledge, 1997, 47.

8 King, 2018, 86.

9 King, 2018, 70.

10 Ibid.

11 Barrett and McIntosh, *The Anti-Social Family*, London: Verso Books, 1991, 42.

12 Kathi Weeks, "Abolition of the Family: The Most Infamous Feminist Proposal," *Feminist Theory*, May 2021.

13 Weeks, "Abolition of the Family," 4.

14 Paul Gilroy, "It's a Family Affair: Black Culture and the Trope of Kinship," in *Small Acts: Thoughts on the Politics of Black Cultures*, London: Serpent's Tail, 1993, 207.

15 Gilroy, "It's a Family Affair," 207.

16 Kay Lindsey, "The Black Woman as a Woman," in Toni Cade Bambara, ed. *The Black Woman: An Anthology,* New York: Washington Square Press, 1970, 106.

17 Pat Parker, "Revolution: It's Not Neat or Pretty or Quick," 238–242 in Moraga and Anzaldúa (eds.), *This Bridge Called My Back: Writings by Radical Women of Color*, New York: Kitchen Table / Women of Color Press, 1981.

18 Lola Olufemi, @lolaolufemi_, February 26, 2020. twitter.com/lolaolufemi_/status/1232597074295840770.

19 Annie Olaloku-Teriba, @annie_etc_, November 14, 2021. twitter.com/annie_etc_/status/1459982438856380432.

20 Fred Moten and Stefano Harney, *the undercommons: Fugitive Planning and Black Study*, Brooklyn: Autonomedia/Minor Compositions, 2013.

3 A Potted History of Family Abolitionism

1 Gay Liberation Front: "Manifesto," 1971, revised 1978, sourcebooks.fordham.edu.

2 Anca Gheaus, 2018, "What Abolishing the Family Would Not Do," *Critical Review of International Social and Political Philosophy*, 21:3, 284–300.

3 See for instance: Gheaus, 2011, "Arguments for Nonparental Care for Children," *Social Theory & Practice* 37(3): 483–509; Véronique Munoz-Dardé, 1999, "Is the Family to Be Abolished Then?" *Proceedings of the Aristotelian Society* 99 (1): 37–56; Sophia Harrison, 2003, "Is Justice within the Family Possible?" *UCL Jurisprudence Rev.* 265. For political philosopher and theorist Miranda Sklaroff's far more illuminating discussion, refer to her 2021 blog post "Mother Wars": politicaltheoryandapeony.com/2021/05/25/mother-wars.

4 On utopian-feminist kitchenless architectural plans in the nineteenth century, see: Dolores Hayden, "Two Utopian Feminists and Their Campaigns for Kitchenless Houses," *Signs* 4(2): 274-290, 1978. On feminist urbanism more generally see: Dolores Hayden, *The Grand Domestic Revolution: A History of Feminist Designs for American Homes, Neighborhoods, and Cities*, Boston: MIT, 1981.

5 Dominic Pettman, "Get Thee to a Phalanstery: or, How Fourier Can Still Teach Us to Make Lemonade," *Public Domain*

Review, 2019. publicdomainreview.org. At one point in this wonderful piece of analysis, Pettman elicits an uncomfortable gasp from one Patreon-dependent reader (me) with the following: "[Fourier's] writings were sponsored by those relatively well-to-do folks interested in his radical theories, à la left-leaning Patreon or Kickstarter patrons."

6 Jonathan Beecher, *Charles Fourier: The Visionary and His World*, University of California Press, 1986, 12.

7 On the Fourierist commune movement, some works to consult: Amy Hart, *Fourierist Communities of Reform: The Social Networks of Nineteenth-Century Female Reformers*, London: Palgrave Macmillan, 2021; Juan Pro, "Thinking of a Utopian Future: Fourierism in Nineteenth-Century Spain," *Utopian Studies* 26(2): 329–348, 2015; Carl Guarneri, *The Utopian Alternative: Fourierism in Nineteenth-Century America*, Ithaca: Cornell UP, 1996; Richard Pankhurst, "Fourierism in Britain," *International Review of Social History* 1(3): 398–432, 1956; Megan Perle Bowman, "Laboring for Global Perfection: The International Dimension of Mid-Nineteenth-Century Fourierism," PhD dissertation, UC Santa Barbara, 2013.

8 Pettman on Fourier: "Clearly, this thinker has never lived in a group house, or been obliged to sit on a committee, for he believed that a rather relentless public existence would, by its own account, bring us, without exception, a profound and unshakable happiness."

9 McKenzie Wark, 2015, "Charles Fourier's Queer Theory," Verso Books, versobooks.com.

10 Pettman 2019.

11 Gareth Stedman Jones and Ian Patterson eds., *The Theory of the Four Movements*, Cambridge: Cambridge University Press, 2016, 128. For more excerpts from texts by Fourier, see: Jonathan Beecher and Richard Bienvenu, eds., *The Utopian Vision of Charles Fourier: Selected Texts on Work, Love, and Passionate Attraction*, Boston: Beacon Press, 1971.

12 Some of the many excellent histories of the imposition upon Indigenous and formerly enslaved populations of "settler sexuality"—including *queer* settler sexuality—and the family are:

Kim TallBear, "The US-Dakota War and Failed Settler Kinship," *Anthropology News*, Vol 57, issue 9, 2016; Priya Kandaswamy, *Domestic Contradictions: Race and Gendered Citizenship from Reconstruction to Welfare Reform*, Durham: Duke University Press, 2021; Nick Estes, *Our History is the Future: Standing Rock Versus the Dakota Access Pipeline, and the Long Tradition of Indigenous Resistance*, New York: Verso, 2019; Mark Rifkin, *When Did Indians Become Straight?: Kinship, the History of Sexuality, and Native Sovereignty*, Oxford: Oxford University Press, 2011; and Scott L. Morgensen, *Spaces between Us: Queer Settler Colonialism and Indigenous Decolonization*, Minneapolis: University of Minnesota Press, 2011.

13 Kim TallBear, "Disrupting Settlement, Sex, and Nature," Future Imaginary Lecture Series, Montréal-Concordia, transcript archived at Indigenous Futures, 2017, indigenousfutures.net.

14 Raymond Fogelson, "On the 'Petticoat Government' of the Eighteenth-Century Cherokee," in Jordan and Swarts (eds.), *Personality and the Cultural Construction of Society*, Tuscaloosa: University of Alabama Press, 1990.

15 See for instance: Mark Rifkin, When Did the Indians Become Straight? Kinship, the History of Sexuality, and Native Sovereignty, Oxford: Oxford University Press, 2010.

16 Lillian Faderman, *Woman: The American History of an Idea*, New Haven: Yale University Press, 2022, 43. Pages 41–43 of Faderman's history address the Code of Handsome Lake.

17 See for instance: Driskill, Finney, Gilley and Morgensen, eds., *Queer Indigenous Studies: Critical Interventions in Theory, Politics, and Literature*, University of Arizona Press, 2011. Regarding the male breast-feeding, specifically, consult: Elspeth Martini, "'Visiting Indians,' Nursing Fathers, and Anglo-American Empires in the Post–War of 1812 Western Great Lakes," *The William and Mary Quarterly* 78(3): 459–490, 2021.

18 Lou Cornum, "Desiring the Tribe," *Pinko*, October 15, 2019. pinko.online.

19 Tera Hunter, *Bound in Wedlock: Slave and Free Black Marriage in the Nineteenth Century*, Cambridge: Harvard, 2017; Katherine Franke, *Wedlocked: The Perils of Marriage Equality*,

New York: NYU, 2015; Brenda Stevenson, "Slave Family and Housing," in *Black and White*, ed. Ted Ownby, Jackson: University of Mississippi, 1993.

20 Cathy Cohen, "Punks, Bulldaggers, and Welfare Queens: The Radical Potential of Queer Politics?" *GLQ* 3 (4): 437–465, 1977; Alexis Pauline Gumbs, "We Can Learn to Mother Ourselves: The Queer Survival of Black Feminism 1968–1996," Duke University, PhD dissertation, dukespace.lib.duke.edu, 2010.

21 J. M. Allain, 2014, "Infanticide as Slave Resistance: Evidence from Barbados, Jamaica, and Saint-Domingue," *Inquiries Journal/Student Pulse* 6.04.

22 O'Brien, M. E., "To Abolish the Family," *Endnotes*, vol. 5, 2020, 375.

23 Weeks summarizes Tera Hunter's findings on the "double-edged sword" of marriage (as experienced by newly emancipated slaves) as follows: "On the one hand, [marriage] certainly offered some legal and economic protections. On the other hand, it was administered by the Freedmen's Bureau as a means both to constitute the nuclear family as the principal labour force of family farming that enabled the transition from the plantation system to sharecropping, and to free the government of further responsibilities toward formerly enslaved people. It represented another mode of bondage within a relationship founded in property rights." Kathi Weeks (2021) 4.; citing Tera Hunter, *Bound in Wedlock: Slave and Free Black Marriage in the Nineteenth Century*, Cambridge: Harvard, 2017, 222, 234, 304.

24 On the man-in-the-house rule, see: Wilson Sherwin and Frances Fox Piven (2019) "The Radical Feminist Legacy of the National Welfare Rights Organization," *WSQ* 47(3–4): 135–153.

25 Saidiya Hartman, *Wayward Lives, Beautiful Experiments: Intimate Histories of Riotous Black Girls, Troublesome Women, and Queer Radicals*, New York: Norton, 2020.

26 "To Abolish the Family," 376.

27 Joseph Déjacque, "The Revolutionary Question" (1948), translated by Paul Sharkey, in *Disruptive Elements: The Extremes of French Anarchism*, Creative Commons: Ardent Press, 2014.

28 On Robert Owen's "New Lanark" cooperative experiment, see: Barbara Taylor, *Eve and the New Jerusalem: Socialism and Feminism in the Nineteenth Century*, London: Virago Press, 1983.

29 On this relationship, see for instance this discussion by an avowed kibbutznik: Avraham Yassour, 1983, "Communism and Utopia: Marx, Engels, and Fourier," *Studies in Soviet Thought* 26(3): 217–227.

30 Karl Marx and Friedrich Engels, ed. C. J. Arthur, 1970, *The German Ideology*, New York: International Publishers, 50.

31 Karl Marx and Friedrich Engels, *The Communist Manifesto*.

32 Richard Weikart, 1994, "Marx, Engels, and the Abolition of the Family," *History of European Ideas* 18(5): 657–672, 669.

33 Gleeson, Jules Joanne, and Kate Doyle Griffiths, "Kinderkommunismus: A Feminist Analysis of the 21st-Century Family and a Communist Proposal for Its Abolition," *Ritual* magazine / Subversion, 2015, isr.press/Griffiths_Gleeson_ Kinderkommunismus/index.html.

34 China Miéville, *A Spectre Haunting*, London: Head of Zeus, 2022.

35 Alexandra Kollontai, 1971 [1920], "Communism and the Family," in *Selected Writings of Alexandra Kollontai*, ed. Alix Holt, London: Allison & Busby.

36 Hardt, Michael, 2017. "Red Love," *South Atlantic Quarterly*, 116 (4), 792.

37 My facts are mainly gathered from: Cathy Porter, *Alexandra Kollontai: A Biography*, London: Virago, 1980.

38 Selected Writings of Alexandra Kollontai, 291.

39 Kollontai, 1971 [1926], *The Autobiography of a Sexually Emancipated Communist Woman*, ed. Iring Fetscher, transl. Salvador Attansio. New York: Herder and Herder, 38.

40 In "Alexandra Kollontai and the Utopian Imagination in the Russian Revolution" (2017), MD Steinberg defends Alexandra's erotic and emotional utopianism in the following striking terms: "She explored the possibility of a communist society that would allow humanity to leap across the *zapovednyi rubezh* (forbidden border) of normative economic laws and necessity into a

world of freedom." *Vestnik of Saint Petersburg University – History* 62(3): 436–448. The collection *Red Love* is edited by Michele Masucci, Maria Lind, and Joanna Warsza (Berlin: Sternberg Press).

41 Dora García, *Love with Obstacles (Amor Rojo)*, Berlin: k-verlag, 2020.

42 Dora García, "Revolution, Fulfill Your Promise!" at Amant Foundation, Brooklyn, NY, Feb. 5–Apr 17, 2022. Two films by García were screened: *Si Pudiera Desear Algo (If I Could Wish for Something)*, 2021, and *Love Without Obstacles*, 2020, both produced by Auguste Orts. More information can be found at amant.org; and in Liza Featherstone's essay about the exhibition, "A New Generation of Radicals Is Rediscovering Alexandra Kollontai," *Jacobin*, March 31, 2022, jacobinmag. com. See also Featherstone, "Eros for the People: Alexandra Kollontai's Sex-Positive Bolshevism," *Lux*, Issue 1, January 2021. lux-magazine.com.

43 Hardt, 2017. "Red Love," 789. Hardt specifies that Lenin's comment—reported by Kollontai's friend and official Soviet biographer Anna Itkina—is cited in Cathy Porter, 1980, *Alexandra Kollontai: The Lonely Struggle of the Woman Who Defied Lenin*, The Dial Press, 1980, 337.

44 At the top of my list of writings on Firestone is: Madeline Lane-McKinley, "The Dialectic of Sex, after the Post-1960s," *Cultural Politics* 15(3): 331–342, 2019, in which Madeline argues that the *Dialectic* should be read as part of the SF wave that includes Piercy, Delany, Butler, and Le Guin: "*The Dialectic of Sex* has been problematically positioned as exemplary of the second-wave radical feminist canon, rather than as its first extensive immanent critique." Also indispensable are Victoria Margree, *Neglected or Misunderstood: The Radical Feminism of Shulamith Firestone*, London: Zer0 Books, 2018; and Kathi Weeks, "The Vanishing Dialectic: Shulamith Firestone and the Future of the Feminist 1970s," *South Atlantic Quarterly* 114 (4): 735–754, 2015. I too have at this point published several tearfully loving as well as scathing tributes to Firestone, opposing the profound racism of Chapter 5

(and whiteness of the project in general) while reading her as a proto-trans cyborgian utopianist: Sophie Lewis, "Shulamith Firestone Wanted to Abolish Nature—We Should, Too," *The Nation*, July 14, 2021, thenation.com; Sophie Lewis, "Low-Tech Grassroots Ectogenesis," *brand new life*, April 2, 2021, brand-new-life.org; and Sophie Lewis, "Disloyal Children of Shulamith Firestone: Updating Gestational Utopianism for the Twenty-First Century," *Interference* journal, vol. 2, 2021. I teach an online course on *The Dialectic*, open to all, at the Brooklyn Institute for Social Research: thebrooklyninstitute.com.

45 Firestone, Shulamith, *The Dialectic of Sex: The Case for Feminist Revolution*, London: Verso, 2012 [1970].

46 Firestone was, of course, unsparing: "Summerhill is no 'radical' approach to child-rearing—it is a liberal one. Neill, a kindly and decent sort of schoolmaster ... has set up a small retreat for those victims of our present system whose parents have the money and liberal views to send them there." *The Dialectic of Sex*, 216.

47 *The Dialectic of Sex*, 215.

48 For a history of the ectogenetic fantasy and my thoughts on a possible gestator-led BioBag revolution, see: Sophie Lewis, "Do Electric Sheep Dream of Water Babies?" *Logic*, 8, August 3, 2019, logicmag.io.

49 *The Dialectic of Sex*, 242.

50 Linda Gordon, "Functions of the Family," *WOMEN: A Journal of Liberation*, 1(2): 20–23, 1969.

51 Sophie Lewis, "Shulamith Firestone Wanted to Abolish Nature—We Should, Too," 2021.

52 Toni Cade's 1970 anthology *The Black Woman* contained several anti-family pieces (notably by Audre Lorde and Kay Lindsey). In February 1970, five hundred women came together for the Women's Liberation Conference at Ruskin College, Oxford, many speakers expressing the desire—and central tenet of feminism—that children "liberate themselves from us [the parents/ adults]." For perspectives from the wreckage that was the early Eighties, see Lynne Segal, ed. *What Is to Be Done About the*

Family? Harmondsworth: Penguin, 1983. Amid the global backlash, Kate Millett only grew more radical on children's liberation, writing in 1984 that desexualization "is how adults control children" ("Beyond Politics: Children and Sexuality," in *Pleasure and Danger* ed. Carole Vance, Routledge).

53 Kate Millett, *Sexual Politics*, 33.

54 Cheryl Clarke, "Lesbianism: An Act of Resistance," in Moraga and Anzaldúa (eds.), *This Bridge Called My Back: Writings by Radical Women of Color*, New York: Kitchen Table / Women of Color Press, 1981, 141–151.

55 Kathi Weeks, "Abolition of the Family: The Most Infamous Feminist Proposal," *Feminist Theory*, May 2021.

56 Ellen Willis, "The Family: Love It or Leave It," *The Village Voice*, September 17, 1979, villagevoice.com.

57 "Red-brown" here is a reference to a sadly not-uncommon "dirtbag left" trajectory, in this case exemplified by the British philosopher and self-described "edgelady" Nina Power, a committed anti-trans reactionary once known as a Marxist feminist, who in 2022 published a piece entitled "Why We Need the Patriarchy" in *Compact*, an online platform devoted to anti-liberalism (also known as the "third way," or left-right, or red and brown—as in, brownshirt—conservativism). The piece in question outlines the pro-patriarchy argument of Power's book *What Do Men Want?: Masculinity and Its Discontents*, published by Allen Lane.

58 Lynne Segal (ed.) *What is to be done about the Family?—Crisis in the Eighties*, Penguin Books / Socialist Society, 1983.

59 Barrett and McIntosh, 1991, 80.

60 Barrett and McIntosh, 1991, 171.

61 Two prominent examples of this walking-back: "Women's Lib is not trying to destroy the American family" (Gloria Steinem); "Feminists have not tried to 'destroy the family.' We just thought the family was such a good idea that men might want to get involved in it too." (Barbara Ehrenreich).

62 For a critique of the positioning of "hate" as the enemy of humanity (via an account of my own mobbing, online, by anti-abortionists), see: Sophie Lewis, "Hello to My Haters: Tucker

Carlson's Mob and Me," *Dissent*, 2020. dissentmagazine.org. A wide range of Catholic populists and what Richard Seymour calls "normie" socialists reacted to the phrase "family abolition," or to my book *Full Surrogacy Now: Feminism Against Family*—or at least its title—with real hatred, and that is as it should be. A handful of examples: Mary Harrington, "Return of the Cyborgs," *First Things*, January 11, 2022; Angela Nagle, "Products of Gestational Labor," *The Lamp*, 2020; Michael McCaffrey, "The woke left are demonizing parents and want to abolish the family: It's the intellectual equivalent of a toddler's tantrum," *RT*, 2020; Kimberly Ellis, "Family love is the foundation of civilization," *MercatorNet*, 2021; and Freddie De Boer's substack (freddiedeboer.substack.com), December 29, 2021.

63 Firestone's hit-or-miss (but often hit) radical-feminist Marxism explored the materiality behind the ostensibly psychological cliché "that women live for love and men for work"—the twenty-first century twist on this being, as Kathi Weeks notes, that we must *all* now love our work and even be *in love with* work. On some of the revolutionary (anti-)love and anti-work traditions in feminism see: Jennifer C. Nash, "Practicing Love: Black Feminism, Love-Politics, and Post-Intersectionality," *Meridians* 11 (2): 1–24, 2011; and Kathi Weeks, "Down with Love: Feminist Critique and the New Ideologies of Work," *Women's Studies Quarterly*, 45(3 & 4): 37–58, 2017.

64 *The Dialectic of Sex*, 90.

65 Susan Faludi, "Death of a Revolutionary," *The New Yorker*, April 8, 2013. newyorker.com.

66 Told to me by Lori Hiris. I am indebted to Hiris for her willingness to disagree with me and speak with me at length on the phone about Firestone's later life.

67 Shulamith Firestone, *Airless Spaces*, Los Angeles: Semiotext(e), 1998.

68 Some of the many tributes were collected by Dayna Tortorici for *n+1*: "In Memoriam: On Shulamith Firestone", *n+1*, issue 5, Winter 2013. nplusonemag.com.

69 Adrienne Rich, *Of Woman Born: Motherhood as Experience and Institution*, New York: Norton, 1986. The Canadian

scholar of "matricentric feminism" Andrea O'Reilly has argued—for instance in her edited collection *From Motherhood to Mothering: The Legacy of Adrienne Rich's* Of Woman Born, New York: SUNY Press, 2004—that the principle of "mothering against motherhood" was Rich's fundamental political legacy. I have attempted to theorize a transfeminist, family-abolitionist expansion of this dialectic. See: Lewis, Sophie, "Mothering against motherhood: doula work, xenohospitality and the idea of the momrade," *Feminist Theory* (Online First), January 10, 2022. doi.org/10.1177/14647001211059520. An earlier version of that essay was published in *Salvage Quarterly* in 2020.

70 Audre Lorde, in "Eye to Eye: Black Women, Hatred, and Anger," *Sister Outsider: Essays and Speeches*, Berkeley: Crossing Press, 1984, 173.

71 Michael Bronski, "When Gays Wanted to Liberate Children," *Boston Review*, June 8, 2018. bostonreview.net.

72 On the various arcs of Gay Liberation, including attention to the material or classed conditions of possibility for insurgent queerness, the history of radical-feminist male gay "effeminism" and the drivers of the male Gay movement's overall de-effeminization, see for instance: Emily Hobson, *Lavender and Red: Liberation and Solidarity in the Gay and Lesbian Left*, Berkeley: University of California Press, 2016; Sherry Wolf, *Sexuality and Socialism: History, Politics, and Theory of LGBT Liberation*, London: Haymarket, 2009; Alan Sears, "Queer Anti-Capitalism: What's Left of Lesbian and Gay Liberation?" *Science & Society*, 69(1): 92–112, 2005; John D'Emilio "Capitalism and Gay Identity," in *Culture, Society and Sexuality*, London: Routledge, (1983 [2006]); David Paternotte, "Tracking the Demise of Gay Liberation Ideals," *Sexualities* 17(1/2): 121–138, 2014; and Jeffrey Edwards, "AIDS, Race, and the Rise and Decline of a Militant Oppositional Lesbian and Gay Politics in the US," *New Political Science*, 22:4, 485–506, 2000.

73 On this history, see e.g., *Screaming Queens: The Riot at Compton's Cafeteria* (2005) dir. Victor Silverman and Susan

Stryker, 57min; and Susan Stryker, *Transgender History*, New York: Seal Press, 2008.

74 On STAR House, see: Stephan Cohen, *The Gay Liberation Youth Movement in New York: "An Army of Lovers Cannot Fail,"* New York: Routledge, 2007; "Sylvia Rivera" in the archives of Zagria (A Gender Variance Who's Who), zagria. blogspot.com; the website of Reina Gossett, reinagossett.com; the zine put out by Untorelli Press, *Street Transvestite Action Revolutionaries: Survival, Revolt, And Queer Antagonist Struggle*, 2013; and Leslie Feinberg, "Street Transvestite Action Revolutionaries," *Workers World*, 2006, workers.org.

75 Carl Wittman, "Refugees from Amerika: A Gay Manifesto," 1970, historyisaweapon.com.

76 For more on these alliances, consult: Abram Lewis, "'We Are Certain of Our Own Insanity': Antipsychiatry and the Gay Liberation Movement, 1968–1980," *Journal of the History of Sexuality* 25(1): 83–113, 2016.

77 Quoted in: Jacques Girard, *Le mouvement homosexuel en France 1945–1980*, Paris: Syros, 1981. For more on the family abolitionism of FHAR, I recommend *F.H.A.R.*, a short documentary directed by Carole Roussopoulos (1971) 26min. mubi. com.

78 Gay Liberation Front: "Manifesto," 1971, revised 1978, sourcebooks.fordham.edu.

79 The ten-point list of demands, which begins "Boston GLF urges that the following principles be incorporated in the 1972 Democratic Party Platform," is reproduced at the end of Michael Bronski's essay "When Gays Wanted to Liberate Children."

80 For more on children's liberation, consult: Shulamith Firestone, *The Dialectic of Sex*; Joan Chatfield-Taylor, "A Child's View of Kids' Lib," *San Francisco Chronicle*, November 23, 1976; David Gottlieb, ed. *Children's Liberation*, Englewood Cliffs: Prentice Hall, 1973; Richard Farson, *Birthrights*, New York: Macmillan, 1974; Beatrice Gross and Ronald Gross, eds., *The Children's Rights Movement: Overcoming the Oppression of Young People*, New York: Anchor Books, 1977; John McMurtry, "The Case for Children's Liberation," *Interchange*

10(3): 10–28, 1979; Kate Millett and M. Blasius, "Sexual revolution and the liberation of children," *The Age Taboo: Gay Male Sexuality, Power and Consent*, 1981; Isobelle Barrett Meyering, "Liberating Children: The Australian Women's Liberation Movement and Children's Rights in the 1970s," *Lilith*, 19: 60–75. 2013.

81 Alexis Pauline Gumbs reflects powerfully on this moment and its ripples in "m/other ourselves: A Black queer feminist genealogy for radical mothering," *Revolutionary Mothering: Love on the Front Lines*, eds. Gumbs, Williams, and Martens, Oakland: PM Press, 2016; as well as in her PhD dissertation " 'We Can Learn To Mother Ourselves': The Queer Survival of Black Feminism," Duke University, 2010. dukespace.lib.duke.edu.

82 For information on one childcare collective local to me, visit: Philly Childcare Collective, phillychildcarecollective.com. For the website of one contemporary network drawing on the legacies of Gay Power and Women's Liberational male childcare collectives, visit: The Intergalactic Conspiracy of Childcare Collectives, or ICCC, intergalactic-childcare.weebly.com.

83 Some resources on Wages for Housework include: Selma James, *Sex, Race and Class: The Perspective of Winning*, PM Press, 2012; Mariarosa Dalla Costa, *Family, Welfare, and the State: Between Progressivism and the New Deal* (2nd edition), Philadelphia: Common Notions, 2021 [1983]; and Louise Toupin, *Wages for Housework: A History of an International Feminist Movement, 1972–77*, London: Pluto Press, 2018; Silvia Federici and Arlen Austin, eds. *Wages for Housework: The New York Committee 1972–1977: History, Theory, Documents*, Oakland: PM Press, 2017.

84 Silvia Federici, Revolution at Point Zero: Housework, Reproduction, and Feminist Struggle, PM Press, 2012, 3.

85 Silvia Federici, *Wages Against Housework*, Power of Women Collective and Falling Wall Press, 1975.

86 For analysis and history of the NWRO: Wilson Sherwin and Frances Fox Piven (2019) "The Radical Feminist Legacy of the National Welfare Rights Organization," *WSQ* 47(3-4): 135–153; Holloway Sparks (2016) "When Dissident Citizens Are Militant

Mamas: Intersectional Gender and Agonistic Struggle in Welfare Rights Activism," *Politics and Gender* 12(4): 623–47; Mary Triece (2013) *Tell It Like It Is: Women in the National Welfare Rights Movement*, Columbia: University of South Carolina; Premilla Nadasen (2011) *Rethinking the Welfare Rights Movement*, New York: Routledge; Felicia Kornbluh (2007) *The Battle for Welfare Rights: Politics and Poverty in Modern America*, Philadelphia: University of Pennsylvania; Annelise Orleck (2006) *Storming Caesar's Palace: How Black Mothers Fought Their Own War on Poverty*, Boston: Beacon Press; Premilla Nadasen (2005) *Welfare Warriors: The Welfare Rights Movement in the United States*, New York: Routledge; Guida West (1998) "Women in the Welfare Rights Movement: Reform or Revolution?" 91–108 in *Women and Revolution: Global Expressions*, ed. Marie Diamond, Dordrecht: Springer.

87 King, "Abolishing Moynihan's Negro Family," 77.

88 Johnnie Tillmon, "Welfare is a Women's Issue," *Ms.*, Spring 1972, msmagazine.com.

89 Sherwin and Piven, "The Radical Feminist Legacy of the National Welfare Rights Organization."

90 The discomfited, reluctantly awe-stricken *NYT* reporter characterized the demeanor of the "welfare libbers" Mrs. Odessa Singleton, Mrs. Irene Gibbs, and Mrs. Rose Thomas as a "combination of schoolgirls on an outing and a combat-tested guerrilla force in the midst of the enemy camp." Richard Rogin, "Now It's Welfare Lib," *The New York Times*, September 27, 1970, 31, nytimes.com.

91 Kornbluh 2007, 1.

92 Beulah Sanders, "Speech to NCC, Houston, Dec 1972," Guida West Papers, Smith College Archives, Box 11, folder 1, transcript. Cited in Colleen Wessel-McCoy (2019) " 'If we fail in our struggle, Christianity will have failed': Beulah Sanders, Welfare Rights, and the Church," *Kairos Center*, kairoscenter.org.

93 "Politics Theory Other" with Alex Doherty, especially episodes #35 ("Full Surrogacy Now") and #102 ("What Covid-19 reveals about the family"). Visit: soundcloud.com/poltheory-other or patreon.com/poltheoryother.

94 Daniel Denvir, "Abolish the Family with Sophie Lewis," *The Dig*, July 11, 2019, thedigradio.com.

95 Kim Brooks, "Parenting in Utopia," *The Cut*, January 11, 2022, thecut.com; Katie Tobin, "Why Young People Are Turning to Platonic Marriages: Abolishing the Family," *Huck*, January 13, 2022, huckmag.com; Marie Solis, "We Can't Have a Feminist Future Without Abolishing the Family," *Vice*, February 20, 2020, vice.com; Jessica Weisberg, "Can Surrogacy Remake the World?" *The New Yorker*, December 11, 2019, newyorker.com; David Brooks, "The Nuclear Family Was a Mistake," *The Atlantic*, March 15, 2020, theatlantic.com. For an example of a communist feminist writing on family abolition in a mainstream literary magazine, see Madeline Lane-McKinley, "Unthinking the Family," *LA Review of Books*, June 10, 2019, lareviewofbooks.org.

96 For an understanding of what this emerging field entails, readers should begin with the writings of Jules Joanne Gleeson (for instance, in *Hypocrite Reader* and *Blind Field Journal*), or by perusing the following three extraordinary anthologies: *We Want It All: An Anthology of Radical Trans Poetics*, ed. Kay Gabriel and Andrea Abi-Karam, Brooklyn: Nightboat Books, 2020; *Transgender Marxism*, ed. Jules Gleeson and Elle O'Rourke, London: Pluto Press, 2021; and *Las Degeneradas Trans Acaban Con la Familia*, ed. Ira Hybris, Madrid: Kaótica Libros, 2022.

97 Jules Joanne Gleeson, and Kate Doyle Griffiths, "Kinderkommunismus: A Feminist Analysis of the 21st-Century Family and a Communist Proposal for Its Abolition," *Ritual* magazine / Subversion, 2015.

98 King, Tiffany Lethabo, "Black 'Feminisms' & Pessimism: Abolishing Moynihan's Negro Family," *Theory & Event* 21 (1): 68–87, 2018.

99 Sophie Lewis, "The Family Lottery," *Dissent*, Summer 2021. dissentmagazine.org; Sophie Lewis, "Low-Tech Grassroots Ectogenesis," *brand new life*, April 2, 2021. brand-new-life.org; Sophie Lewis, "Houses Into Homes," *UCHRI Foundry*, July 2020. uchri.org; Sophie Lewis, "Mothering Against the World:

Momrades Against Motherhood," *Salvage*, September 18, 2020. salvage.zone; Sophie Lewis, "Covid-19 Is Straining the Concept of the Family. Let's Break It." *The Nation*, June 3, 2020. thenation.com; Sophie Lewis, "The Satanic Death-Cult is Real," *Commune*, August 28, 2019.

100 *viz.* Gleeson's contribution to the "Full Surrogacy Now Mini-symposium" at the Verso Blog, 4 June 2019, versobooks.com.

101 Katie Stone, "Strange Children: Childhood, Utopianism, Science Fiction," PhD thesis, Birkbeck, University of London, 2021. See also Katie Stone's family-abolitionist essay on vampires, "Hungry for Utopia: An Antiwork Reading of Bram Stoker's *Dracula*," *Utopian Studies*, 32 (2):296–310, 2021.

102 Alva Gotby, "They Call it Love: Wages for Housework and Emotional Reproduction" PhD thesis, University of West London, 2019 (repository.uwl.ac.uk); Alva Gotby, "Liberated Sex: Firestone on Love and Sexuality," MAI, April 18, 2018, maifeminism.com.

103 Sophie Silverstein, "Family Abolition Isn't about Ending Love and Care. It's About Extending It to Everyone," *openDemocracy*, April 24, 2020, opendemocracy.net.

104 Zoe Belinsky, "Gender and Family Abolition as an Expansive and not Reductive Process," *Medium*, September 11, 2019, medium.com.

105 Alyson Escalante, "The Family is Dead, Long Live the Family," *Cosmonaut*, March 11, 2020.

106 "Abolish the Family!," Red May 2020, with Kathi Weeks, Sarah Jaffe, M. E. O'Brien, Will McKeithen, and Sophie Lewis, youtube.com.

107 Kathi Weeks, "Abolition of the Family: The Most Infamous Feminist Proposal,," *Feminist Theory*, May 2021.

108 "What is Family Abolition" with Sophie Lewis, The Brooklyn Institute for Social Research, thebrooklyninstitute.com.

109 M. E. O'Brien and Eman Abdelhadi, *Everything for Everyone: An Oral History of the New York Commune, 2052–2072*, Philadelphia: Common Notions, 2022.

110 O'Brien, "Communizing Care."

4 Comrades Against Kinship

1 Barrett and McIntosh, *The Anti-Social Family*, 158.

2 "These "Adults Moved Back In with Their Parents During the Pandemic. But Did They Regret It?" *The Guardian*, October 10, 2021. theguardian.com.

3 The name "Camp JTD" was adopted temporarily in honor of a deceased comrade, James Talib-Dean Campbell, a co-founder of the local Workers Revolutionary Collective.

4 The life of Jennifer Bennetch, Philadelphia's finest eviction-busting abolitionist powerhouse (and scourge of the Philadelphia Housing Authority) was stolen by COVID-19 in 2022, when Jen was only thirty-six years old. For a timeline of the encampments Bennetch co-organized during the uprisings of 2020, refer to the anthology *How We Stay Free: Notes on a Black Uprising*, eds. Christopher R. Rogers, Fajr Muhammad, and the Paul Robeson House & Museum, Philadelphia: Common Notions, 2022.

5 Camp Maroon was the process that prompted the observation "*What Makes a House a Home? Unfortunately, Revolution Alone.*" Sophie Lewis, "Houses into Homes," UCHRI Foundry, July 2020. uchri.org.

6 For more on the unhoused people's Philadelphia encampment of 2020: It's Going Down, 2021, "Squatting, Rebellion, Movement: An Interview With Philadelphia Housing Action," itsgoingdown.org; Madison Gray, 2020, "How The Philly #HousingNow Encampment Movement Prompts Us to Reimagine A Right to Contract," lpeproject.org; Chris Gelardi, 2020, "A Movement for Housing Justice Is Camped Out on Philly Streets," *The Nation*, thenation.com.

7 M. E. O'Brien, "Six Steps to Abolish the Family," *Commune*, December 30, 2019. communemag.com.

8 On the coordinated Christian-nationalist assault on trans children and abortion rights across America in Spring 2022: Jules Gill-Peterson, "We, the Abuser State," *Sad Brown Girl* (substack), February 23, 2022, sadbrowngirl.substack.com; Melissa Gira Grant, "The Law Alone Can't Halt the Christian Right's Crusade Against Abortion and LGBTQ Rights," *The New Republic*, April 6, 2022, newrepublic.com.

9 Ruth Wilson Gilmore, "Abolition Feminism," 161–178 in Brenna Bhandar and Rafeef Ziadah, *Revolutionary Feminisms: Conversations on Collection Action and Radical Thought*, London: Verso, 2020.

10 Ruth Wilson Gilmore, ed. Naomi Murakawa, *Change Everything: Racial Capitalism and the Case for Abolition*, London: Haymarket, 2022.

11 Speaking of "*our maid is part of the family*," readers may wish to look at my 2021 essay on wages against housework, killer nannies, Cinderella/Pamela narratives, and the depiction of commodified housework in a handful of bestselling novels and memoirs of the 2019–2021 period—*Women's Work* by Megan K. Stack, *The Perfect Nanny* by Leïla Slimani, and *Maid* by Stephanie Land—as well as in the Netflix tv mini-series *Maid* (dir. Molly Smith Metzler). The lecture version of this piece, "They Say It is Love," which I presented in March 2022 in the University of London's *Centre for the Study of Contemporary Women's Writing Seminar Series* can be viewed on the "School of Advanced Study" channel on YouTube: " 'WHO CARES' In Contemporary Women's Writing & Film, Session 1: Care, (Geo)politics, and the Social," youtube.com. Sophie Lewis, "How Domestic Labor Robs Women of Their Love," *Boston Review*, October 28, 2021, bostonreview.net.

12 Donna Haraway, *Modest_Witness@Second_Millennium. Female Man_Meets_OncoMouse: Feminism and Technoscience*, New York: Routledge, 1997, 265.

13 On the encounter between *Full Surrogacy Now* and Adele Clark and Donna Haraway's *Making Kin Not Population*, see Jenny Turner, "Nothing Natural," *The London Review of Books*, 42(2), January 23, 2020, lrb.co.uk.; In her review, Turner discusses my essay on Haraway's 2017 monograph *Staying with the Trouble: Making Kin in the Chthulucene*, in which I rail against what I saw, in 2017, as its betrayal of the Cyborg Manifesto. See Sophie Lewis, "Cthulhu plays no role for me," *Viewpoint*, May 8, 2017. viewpointmag.com.

14 Barrett and McIntosh, 1991, 159.

15 McKenzie Wark, "Make Kith, Not Kin!" *Public Seminar*, June 24, 2016. publicseminar.org.

16 Patricia Hill Collins, "It's All In the Family: Intersections of Gender, Race and Nation," *Hypatia* 13(3): 62–82, 1998, 77.

17 Ellen Willis, "The Family: Love It or Leave It," *The Village Voice*, September 17, 1979, villagevoice.com/2019/03/08/the-family-love-it-or-leave-it

18 Lou Cornum, "Desiring the Tribe," *Pinko* magazine, October 15, 2019, pinko.online.

19 Kathi Weeks, "Abolition of the Family: The Most Infamous Feminist Proposal," *Feminist Theory*, May 2021.

20 Lola Olufemi, *Experiments in Imagining Otherwise*, London: Hajar Press, 2021, 137.

21 *Experiments in Imagining Otherwise*, 138.

Acknowledgments

This book's debt is first to Rosie Warren—for everything. To everyone at *Salvage Quarterly*, and everyone at Verso, who nurtured this little book.

And then, this book's debt is to the one I wake up for and am mind-melded with. And the one for whom I puddle. Furthermore: celui que j'ai connu depuis toujours, avec le tatouage en safflower. The sisters in terror Barnacle and Robespierre. My friends. My comrades. My reading groups. An meine Mumputz: du fehlst mir.

This book's lifeblood comes from utopians with a small u and communists with a small c, everywhere, on every earth. It has been sustained by those who write letters, and by those who give me the gift, in various mediums, of challenge, criticism, and critique. It has been tutored by those who rope me in to speak (and listen), hook me up with gigs, invite me into their classrooms, branches and zine libraries, put me up on stages, and show me random acts of kindness or solidarity from near or far.

This book's debt is to those who enable me to pay my bills, year after year, supporting me on Patreon or in other material ways. I'd like to give a special mention to the generosity of Sarah Miller, Laurel Rogers, Nick Mitchell, Chloé de Canson, Thomas Strong, Kate Marcus, Grace Lavery, Lisa Duggan, Sarah Sharma, Sarah Skenazy, Emma Pike, Brittany Shannahan, Steve Cipolla, Jess Barbagallo, Natalia Cecire, Jason Prado, Pilar Gonalons-Pons, Aude Fellay, Miranda Iossifidis, Maddie Breeze, Keaton Boyle, Michelle Miller. Maria Garcia Gil, Eve O'Connor, Kate Richardson, and Claire Colebrook.

This book's debt is equally to those, too many to list, who believed in me enough to encourage me, represent me (Ian) or go to bat for me ("team erotic octopus" . . .!). It is to those who translated my texts, commissioned them, edited them, made iris-print broadsheets and zines out of them, re-mixed them, anthologized them, turned them into plays, and, you know, read them.

To the extraordinary participants in seven Brooklyn Institute for Social Research courses thus far: Femonationalism, Who is Feminism For?, What is Family Abolition?, Trans/Queer/Woman, The Dialectic of Sex, The Problem with Work, and Children's Liberation (not to mention BISR itself, which lets me run these). And the revolutionaries involved in The Psychosocial Foundation seminar series on the Family Problem, and its sister journal, *Parapraxis*.

To the revolutionaries whose writings about family abolition are so dear to my heart: Michelle, Tiffany, Kathi, Jules, Kate, Helen, Katie, Alva, Sophie, Madeline, Ira, and everyone else, including those no longer living . . . going back to the Fourierist-feminist urban planners discussed by Dolores Hayden in her work on kitchenlessness.

To M. E., in particular, whose book on family abolition is about to make waves. To my city, and in particular Hannah, Asa, Virgil, Lou, horror club, Egina, Ben, Kelly,

Malina, Julia, Miranda, Will, Bea, Artie, Joseph, Sukaina, Cerise, Paul, Max, and the death doulas. To my diaspora, and in particular Richard, Isabel, Alyssa, Tash, Tash, the Marilyn Appreciation Society, Judy, Marcia, Scot, Jo, Emma, Mathura, Hannah, Alice, Yuan, Dave, Tom, Brittany, Katie, Fiorenza, Greg, Patrizia, Antonia, Wilson, Kyle, Lizzie, Sarah, Sarah, Calix, Milo, Elliot, Petra, Sophie, Rees, Lily, Ryan, Nic, Sarah, Anna, and Mél. Blind Field, Out of the Woods, and all the creatures trying to get free.

Further Reading

Angry Workers of the World, "Insurrection and Production,"
August 29, 2016, angryworkers.org.

Barrett, Michèle, and Mary McIntosh, The Anti-Social Family,
London: Verso Books, 1991.

Beecher, Jonathan, Charles Fourier: The Visionary and his World,
Berkeley and Los Angeles: University of California Press, 1986.

Brenner, Johanna, "Utopian Families," Socialist Register, 36:
133–144, 2000.

Bronski, Michael, "When Gays Wanted to Liberate Children,"
Boston Review, June 8, 2018. bostonreview.net.

Butler, Judith, "Is Kinship Always Already Heterosexual? differences: A Journal of Feminist Cultural Studies, 13(1): 14–44,
2002.

Capper, Beth and Arlen Austin, "Wages for Housework Means
Wages against Heterosexuality: On the Archives of Black Women
for Wages for Housework & Wages Due Lesbians," Gay &
Lesbian Quarterly 24(4): 445–466, 2018.

Care Collective, The Care Manifesto: The Politics of Interdependence,
London: Verso, 2020.

Carter, Julian, The Heart of Whiteness: Normal Sexuality and Race
in America, 1880–1940. Durham, NC: Duke University Press,
2007.

Clements, Barbara, "The Utopianism of the Zhenotdel," Slavic
Review, 51(3): 485–496, 1992.

Cohen, Cathy, "Punks, Bulldaggers, and Welfare Queens: The Radical Potential of Queer Politics?" *GLQ* 3 (4): 437–465, 1977.

Collins, Patricia Hill, "It's All in the Family: Intersections of Gender, Race, and Nation," *Hypatia*, 13(3): 62–82, 1998.

Conrad, Ryan, ed. *Against Equality: Queer Revolution, not Mere Inclusion*, Oakland, CA: AK Press, 2014.

Cooper, David, *The Death of the Family*, London: Penguin, 1972.

Cooper, Melinda, *Family Values: Between Neoliberalism and the New Social Conservatism*, New York: Zone Books, 2017.

Coontz, Stephanie, *The Way We Never Were: American Families and the Nostalgia Trap*, New York: Basic Books, 1992.

Cott, Nancy, *Public Vows: A History of Marriage and the Nation*, Cambridge: Harvard University Press, 2000.

Engels, Frederick, *The Origin of the Family, Private Property and the State*, ed. Michèle Barrett, London: Penguin, 1986.

Federici, Silvia, and Nicole Cox, *Counter-Planning from the Kitchen*, New York: Falling Wall Press. 1975.

Firestone, Shulamith, *The Dialectic of Sex: The Case for Feminist Revolution*, New York: William Morrow, 1970.

Fortunati, Leopoldina, *The Arcane of Reproduction: Housework, Prostitution, Labor and Capital*, trans. Hilary Creek, Brooklyn: Autonomedia, 1994 [1981].

Fourier, Charles, Jonathan Beecher, and Richard Bienvenu (eds.), *The Utopian Vision of Charles Fourier: Selected Texts on Work, Love, and Passionate Attraction*, Boston: Beacon Press, 1971.

Franke, Katherine, *Wedlocked: The Perils of Marriage Equality*, New York: NYU Press, 2015.

García, Dora, ed. *Love with Obstacles (Amor Rojo)*, Berlin: K-Verlag, 2020.

Gay Liberation Front: "Manifesto," 1971, revised 1978, source-books.fordham.edu.

Gleeson, Jules Joanne, "This Infamous Proposal," *New Socialist*, March 14, 2020, newsocialist.org.

Gleeson, Jules Joanne, and Kate Doyle-Griffiths, "Kinderkommunismus: A Feminist Analysis of the 21st-Century Family and a Communist Proposal for Its Abolition," *Ritual* magazine / *Subversion*, 2015.

Gordon, Linda, "Functions of the Family," *WOMEN: A Journal of Liberation*, 1(2): 20–23. 1969.

Gotby, Alva, "Liberated Sex: Firestone on Love and Sexuality," April 18, 2018, *MAI*, maifeminism.com.

Gumbs, Alexis Pauline, "We Can Learn to Mother Ourselves: The Queer Survival of Black Feminism 1968–1996," Duke University, PhD dissertation, dukespace.lib.duke.edu, 2010.

Gumbs, Alexis Pauline, China Martens, and Mai'a Williams (eds.), *Revolutionary Mothering: Love on the Front Lines*, Oakland, CA: PM Press, 2016.

Hamilton, Jennifer Mae, "The Future of Housework: The Similarities and Differences Between Making Kin and Making Babies," *Australian Feminist Studies* 34(102): 468–489, 2019.

Hardt, Michael, "Red Love," *South Atlantic Quarterly*, 116(4): 781–796, 2017.

Hartman, Saidiya, *Wayward Lives, Beautiful Experiments: Intimate Histories of Riotous Black Girls, Troublesome Women, and Queer Radicals*, New York: Norton, 2020.

Hayden, Dolores, "Two Utopian Feminists and Their Campaigns for Kitchenless Houses," *Signs* 4(2): 274–290, 1978.

Hayden, Dolores, *The Grand Domestic Revolution: A History of Feminist Designs for American Homes, Neighborhoods, and Cities*, Boston: MIT, 1981.

Hester, Helen, *Xenofeminism*, London: Polity, 2018.

Hester, Helen, "Promethean Labors and Domestic Realism," e-flux, September 25, 2017, e-flux.com.

Hester, Helen, interviewed by Anna Engelhardt and Sasha Shestakova, "Helen Hester on Xeno-Solidarity and the Collective Struggle for Free Time," Strelka magazine, July 2020, strelkamag.com.

Humanaesfera, "Against the (New and Old) Familism: Down with the Family!" (English translation), pseudonymous, 2015, reproduced from the Humanaesfera blog at Libcom: libcom.org.

Hunter, Tera, *Bound in Wedlock: Slave and Free Black Marriage in the Nineteenth Century*, Cambridge: Harvard, 2017.

Hybris, Ira, ed. *Las Degeneradas Trans Acaban Con la Familia*, Madrid: Kaótica Libros, 2022.

Jaffe, Sarah, *Work Won't Love You Back: How Devotion to Our Jobs Keeps Us Exploited, Exhausted and Alone,* New York: Hurst, 2021.

King, Tiffany Lethabo, "Black 'Feminisms' and Pessimism: Abolishing Moynihan's Negro Family," *Theory & Event* 21 (1): 68–87, 2018.

Kollontai, Alexandra, *Selected Writings*, trans. and ed. Alix Holt, New York: W.W. Norton, 1977.

Lane-McKinley, Madeline, "The Idea of Children," August 1, 2018. *Blind Field Journal.* blindfieldjournal.com.

Lane-McKinley, Madeline, "Unthinking the Family in Full Surrogacy Now," *LA Review of Books*, June 19, 2019. lareviewofbooks.org.

Lewis, Sophie, "Mothering against Motherhood: Doula Work, Xenohospitality and the Idea of the Momrade," *Feminist Theory* (Online First), January 10, 2022. doi. org/10.1177/14647001211059520.

Lewis, Sophie, "The Family Lottery," *Dissent*, Summer 2021. dissentmagazine.org.

Lewis, Sophie, "Shulamith Firestone Wanted to Abolish Nature—We Should, Too," *The Nation*, July 14, 2021. thenation.com.

Lewis, Sophie, "Houses into Homes," *UCHRI Foundry*, July 2020. uchri.org.

Lewis, Sophie, "Covid-19 Is Straining the Concept of the Family. Let's Break It." *The Nation*, June 3, 2020. thenation.com.

Lewis, Sophie, *Full Surrogacy Now: Feminism Against Family*, London: Verso Books, 2019.

Lewis, Sophie, "The Satanic Death-Cult is Real," *Commune*, 28 August, 2019. communemag.com.

Lewis, Sophie, "Do Electric Sheep Dream of Water Babies?" *Logic*, 8, August 3, 2019, logicmag.io.

Lewis, Sophie, "Cthulhu Plays No Role for Me," *Viewpoint Magazine*, May 8, 2017. viewpointmag.com.

Lindsey, Kay, "The Black Woman as a Woman," in Toni Cade Bambara, ed. *The Black Woman: An Anthology*, New York: Washington Square Press, 1970.

Margree, Vicky, *Neglected or Misunderstood: The Radical Feminism of Shulamith Firestone*, London: Zero, 2018.

Masucci, Michele, Maria Lind, and Joanna Warsza (eds.) *Red Love: A Reader on Alexandra Kollontai*, Berlin: Sternberg Press, 2020.

McMurtry, John, "The Case for Children's Liberation," *Interchange* 10(3): 10–28, 1979.

Mecca, Tommi Avicolli, *Smash the Church, Smash the State! The Early Years of Gay Liberation*, San Francisco: City Lights, 2009.

Meyering, Isobelle Barrett, "Liberating Children: The Australian Women's Liberation Movement and Children's Rights in the 1970s," *Lilith*, 19: 60–75, 2013.

Mieli, Mario, *Towards a Gay Communism*, trans. Evan Calder Williams, London: Pluto, 2018.

Millett, Kate, interview with M. Blasius, "Sexual revolution and the liberation of children," in *Loving Boys, Semiotext(e) Special Intervention Series #2*, 1980, ipce.info.

Merck, Mandy and Stella Sandford, eds. *Further Adventures of the Dialectic of Sex*, London: Palgrave Macmillan, 2010.

Nash, Jennifer, "The Political Life of Black Motherhood," *Feminist Studies*, 44:3, 699–712, 2018.

Nash, Jennifer, "Practicing Love: Black Feminism, Love-Politics, and Post-Intersectionality," *Meridians*, 11(2): 1–24, 2011.

Olufemi, Lola, *Experiments in Imagining Otherwise*, London: Hajar Press, 2021.

O'Brien, M. E., and Eman Abdelhadi, *Everything for Everyone: An Oral History of the New York Commune, 2052–2072*, Philadelphia: Common Notions, 2022.

O'Brien, M. E., "6 Steps to Abolish the Family," *Commune*, December 30, 2019, communemag.com.

O'Brien, M. E., "To Abolish the Family," *Endnotes*, vol. 5, 2020, endnotes.org.uk.

O'Brien, M. E., "Communizing Care," *Pinko*, October 15, 2019, pinko.online.

Parker, Pat, "Revolution: It's Not Neat or Pretty or Quick," 238–242 in Moraga and Anzaldúa (eds.), *This Bridge Called My Back: Writings by Radical Women of Color*, New York: Kitchen Table / Women of Color Press, 1981.

Paternotte, David, "Tracking the demise of gay liberation ideals," *Sexualities* 17(1/2): 121–138, 2014.

Piercy, Marge, *Woman on the Edge of Time*, London: Fawcett, 1976.

Popkin, Jeremy, "Family Ties in Revolutionary Perspective," *Journal of Social History*, 40(4), 2007.

Porter, Cathy, *Alexandra Kollontai: A Biography*, London: Virago, 1980.

Segal, Lynne, ed. *What Is to Be Done About the Family?* Harmondsworth: Penguin, 1983.

Seymour, Richard, "Notes on a Normie Shitstorm," *Salvage Quarterly*, January 27, 2022, salvage.zone.

Sharpe, Christina, "Lose Your Kin," *The New Inquiry*, November 16, 2016, thenewinquiry.com.

Sherwin, Wilson, and Frances Fox Piven, "The Radical Feminist Legacy of the National Welfare Rights Organization," *WSQ* 47(3-4): 135–153, 2019.

Silverstein, Sophie, "Family abolition isn't about ending love and care. It's about extending it to everyone," *openDemocracy*, April 24, 2020.

Spillers, Hortense, 'Mama's Baby, Papa's Maybe: An American Grammar Book,' *diacritics* 17(2):64–81, 1987.

Steinberg, M. D., "Alexandra Kollontai and the Utopian Imagination in the Russian Revolution," *Vestnik of Saint Petersburg University, History* 62(3): 436–448, 2017.

Stone, Katie, "Reciprocal Babymaking is the Future," *Vector*, May 6, 2019, vectorbsfa.com.

TallBear, Kim, "Making Love and Relations Beyond Settler Sex and Family" in Clarke and Haraway (eds.) *Making Kin Not Population*. Chicago: Prickly Paradigm Press, 2017.

Tillmon, Johnnie, "Welfare Is a Women's Issue," *Ms. Magazine*, 1972, msmagazine.com.

Wark, McKenzie, "Make Kith, Not Kin!" *Public Seminar*.

Wark, McKenzie, "Charles Fourier's Queer Theory," Verso Books Blog, 2015, versobooks.com.

Weeks, Kathi, "Abolition of the Family: The Most Infamous Feminist Proposal," *Feminist Theory*, May 2021.

Weeks, Kathi, "The Vanishing Dialectic: Shulamith Firestone and the Future of the Feminist 1970s," *South Atlantic Quarterly* 114 (4): 735–754, 2015.

Week, Kathi, "Down with Love: Feminist Critique and the New Ideologies of Work," *Women's Studies Quarterly*, 45(3 & 4): 37–58, 2017.

Weikart, Richard, "Marx, Engels, and the Abolition of the Family," *History of European Ideas,* 18(5): 657–672, 1994.

Willis, Ellen, "The Family: Love It or Leave It," *New Political Science* 1(4): 49–63, 1980.

Wittman, Carl, "Refugees from Amerika: A Gay Manifesto," 1970, historyisaweapon.com.

About Salvage Editions

Salvage Editions is a collaboration between Verso Books and *Salvage*. Edited by the Salvage Collective, the series publishes writers the editors admire on various topics. Some of these interventions extend and develop arguments initially published in *Salvage*, others are entirely new. As with all *Salvage*'s publishing, Salvage Editions intervenes in the key theoretical and political questions thrown up by our moment in ways both politically incisive and stylistically ambitious and engaged. The Salvage Collective does not believe, put simply, that radical writing should not also strive for beauty.

Since 2015, *Salvage* has been publishing essays, poetry, fiction, and visual art in its print edition, currently published twice a year. In 2020, along with the Salvage Editions book series, the Salvage Collective also began a live online events series in collaboration with Haymarket Books, called Salvage Live.

Over the years and issues, a cluster of concerns has emerged as core to *Salvage*'s project, including global political economy; modern political subjectivity; the social industries; sexuality, race and identity; and eco-socialism.

For more on *Salvage* and for information about subscribing, please go to www.salvage.zone.